Windows 7: New Features

Instructor's Edition

Windows 7: New Features

President, Axzo Press:	Jon Winder
Vice President, Product Development:	Charles G. Blum
Vice President, Operations:	Josh Pincus
Director of Publishing Systems Development:	Dan Quackenbush
Writer:	Brandon Heffernan
Copyeditor:	Catherine Oliver
Keytester:	Cliff Coryea

For more information, go to www.axzopress.com.

Trademarks

ILT Series is a trademark of Axzo Press.

Some of the product names and company names used in this book have been used for identification purposes only and may be trademarks or registered trademarks of their respective manufacturers and sellers.

Disclaimer

We reserve the right to revise this publication and make changes from time to time in its content without notice.

ISBN 10: 1-4260-1816-9
ISBN 13: 978-1-4260-1816-9

Printed in the United States of America

1 2 3 4 5 6 7 8 9 10 GL 11 10 09

Contents

Introduction

After reading this introduction, you will know how to:

A Use ILT Series manuals in general.

B Use prerequisites, a target student description, course objectives, and a skills inventory to properly set students' expectations for the course.

C Set up a classroom to teach this course.

D Get support for setting up and teaching this course.

Topic A: About the manual

ILT Series philosophy

Our goal is to make you, the instructor, as successful as possible. To that end, our manuals facilitate students' learning by providing structured interaction with the software itself. While we provide text to help you explain difficult concepts, the hands-on activities are the focus of our courses. Leading the students through these activities will teach the skills and concepts effectively.

We believe strongly in the instructor-led class. For many students, having a thinking, feeling instructor in front of them will always be the most comfortable way to learn. Because the students' focus should be on you, our manuals are designed and written to facilitate your interaction with the students, and not to call attention to manuals themselves.

We believe in the basic approach of setting expectations, then teaching, and providing summary and review afterwards. For this reason, lessons begin with objectives and end with summaries. We also provide overall course objectives and a course summary to provide both an introduction to and closure on the entire course.

Our goal is your success. We encourage your feedback in helping us to continually improve our manuals to meet your needs.

Manual components

The manuals contain these major components:

- Table of contents
- Introduction
- Units
- Course summary
- Glossary
- Index

Each element is described below.

Table of contents

The table of contents acts as a learning roadmap for you and the students.

Introduction

The introduction contains information about our training philosophy and our manual components, features, and conventions. It contains target student, prerequisite, objective, and setup information for the specific course. Finally, the introduction contains support information.

Units

Units are the largest structural component of the actual course content. A unit begins with a title page that lists objectives for each major subdivision, or topic, within the unit. Within each topic, conceptual and explanatory information alternates with hands-on activities. Units conclude with a summary comprising one paragraph for each topic, and an independent practice activity that gives students an opportunity to practice the skills they've learned.

The conceptual information takes the form of text paragraphs, exhibits, lists, and tables. The activities are structured in two columns, one telling students what to do, the other providing explanations, descriptions, and graphics. Throughout a unit, instructor notes are found in the left margin.

Course summary

This section provides a text summary of the entire course. It is useful for providing closure at the end of the course. The course summary also indicates the next course in this series, if there is one, and lists additional resources students might find useful as they continue to learn about the software.

Glossary

The glossary provides definitions for all of the key terms used in this course.

Index

The index at the end of this manual makes it easy for you and your students to find information about a particular software component, feature, or concept.

Manual conventions

We've tried to keep the number of elements and the types of formatting to a minimum in the manuals. We think this aids in clarity and makes the manuals more classically elegant looking. But there are some conventions and icons you should know about.

Instructor note/icon	Item	Description
	Italic text	In conceptual text, indicates a new term or feature.
	Bold text	In unit summaries, indicates a key term or concept. In an independent practice activity, indicates an explicit item that you select, choose, or type.
	`Code font`	Indicates code or syntax.

	`Longer strings of ▶`
	`code will look ▶`
	`like this.`
		In the hands-on activities, any code that's too long to fit on a single line is divided into segments by one or more continuation characters (▶). This code should be entered as a continuous string of text.

Instructor notes.		In the left margin, provide tips, hints, and warnings for the instructor.
	Select **bold item**	In the left column of hands-on activities, bold sans-serif text indicates an explicit item that you select, choose, or type.
	Keycaps like ENTER	Indicate a key on the keyboard you must press.
Warning icon.		Warnings prepare instructors for potential classroom management problems.
TIPS *Tip icon.*		Tips give extra information the instructor can share with students.
Setup icon.		Setup notes provide a realistic business context for instructors to share with students, or indicate additional setup steps required for the current activity.
Projector icon.		Projector notes indicate that there is a PowerPoint slide for the adjacent content.

Hands-on activities

The hands-on activities are the most important parts of our manuals. They are divided into two primary columns. The "Here's how" column gives short directions to the students. The "Here's why" column provides explanations, graphics, and clarifications. To the left, instructor notes provide tips, warnings, setups, and other information for the instructor only. Here's a sample:

Do it!

A-1: Creating a commission formula

Take the time to make sure your students understand this worksheet. We'll be here a while.

Here's how	Here's why
1 Open Sales	This is an oversimplified sales compensation worksheet. It shows sales totals, commissions, and incentives for five sales reps.
2 Observe the contents of cell F4	F4 = =E4*C_Rate The commission rate formulas use the name "C_Rate" instead of a value for the commission rate.

For these activities, we have provided a collection of data files designed to help students learn each skill in a real-world business context. As students work through the activities, they will modify and update these files. Of course, students might make a mistake and therefore want to re-key the activity starting from scratch. To make it easy to start over, students will rename each data file at the end of the first activity in which the file is modified. Our convention for renaming files is to add the word "My" to the beginning of the file name. In the above activity, for example, students are using a file called "Sales" for the first time. At the end of this activity, they would save the file as "My sales," thus leaving the "Sales" file unchanged. If students make mistakes, they can start over using the original "Sales" file.

In some activities, however, it might not be practical to rename the data file. Such exceptions are indicated with an instructor note. If students want to retry one of these activities, you will need to provide a fresh copy of the original data file.

PowerPoint presentations

Each unit in this course has an accompanying PowerPoint presentation. These slide shows are designed to support your classroom instruction while providing students with a visual focus. Each presentation begins with a list of unit objectives and ends with a unit summary slide. We strongly recommend that you run these presentations from the instructor's station as you teach this course. A copy of PowerPoint Viewer is included, so it is not necessary to have PowerPoint installed on your computer.

The ILT Series PowerPoint add-in

The CD also contains a PowerPoint add-in that enables you to do two things:

- Create slide notes for the class
- Display a control panel for the Flash movies embedded in the presentations

To load the PowerPoint add-in:

1. Copy the Course_ILT.ppa file to a convenient location on your hard drive.
2. Start PowerPoint.
3. Choose Tools, Macro, Security to open the Security dialog box. On the Security Level tab, select Medium (if necessary), and then click OK.
4. Choose Tools, Add-Ins to open the Add-Ins dialog box. Then, click Add New.
5. Browse to and double-click the Course_ILT.ppa file, and then click OK. A message box will appear, warning you that macros can contain viruses.
6. Click Enable Macros. The Course_ILT add-in should now appear in the Available Add-Ins list (in the Add-Ins dialog box). The "x" in front of Course_ILT indicates that the add-in is loaded.
7. Click Close to close the Add-Ins dialog box.

After you complete this procedure, a new toolbar will be available at the top of the PowerPoint window. This toolbar contains a single button labeled "Create SlideNotes." Click this button to generate slide-notes files in both text (.txt) and Excel (.xls) format. By default, these files will be saved to the folder that contains the presentation. If the PowerPoint file is on a CD-ROM or in some other location to which the slide-notes files cannot be saved, you will be prompted to save the presentation to your hard drive and try again.

When you run a presentation and come to a slide that contains a Flash movie, you will see a small control panel in the lower-left corner of the screen. You can use this panel to start, stop, and rewind the movie, or to play it again.

Topic B: Setting student expectations

Properly setting students' expectations is essential to your success. This topic will help you do that by providing:

- Prerequisites for this course
- A description of the target student
- A list of the objectives for the course
- A skills assessment for the course

Course prerequisites

Students taking this course should be familiar with personal computers and the use of a keyboard and a mouse. This course assumes that students are familiar with a previous version of Windows, such as Windows XP or Windows Vista.

Target student

The target student for this course should be comfortable using a Windows PC. Students will get the most out of this course if their goals are to apply their current skills to using Windows 7. Students will learn how to customize the Windows 7 environment, use Jump Lists and gadgets, manage content by using libraries and Windows Explorer, search for content, interact with devices, protect files, troubleshoot problems, and use new privacy and security features in Internet Explorer.

Course objectives

You should share these overall course objectives with your students at the beginning of the day. This will give the students an idea about what to expect, and it will help you identify students who might be misplaced. Students are considered misplaced when they lack the prerequisite knowledge or when they already know most of the subject matter to be covered.

After completing this course, students will know how to:

- Use the new features of the taskbar and Start menu, switch among open files and programs, and move and resize windows.
- Customize the taskbar, Start menu, and notification area, and use Jump Lists and gadgets.
- Create and manage folders and libraries, customize Windows Explorer, edit file metadata, and search the computer for specific content.
- Work with devices, get familiar with Device Stage, and install a local printer.
- Back up and restore files and folders, encrypt a drive by using BitLocker To Go, troubleshoot problems, make older programs compatible with Windows 7, and record steps to allow support staff to resolve a problem efficiently.
- Customize security and privacy settings in Internet Explorer, manage their browsing data, and use the new InPrivate Browsing and Filtering features.

Skills inventory

Use the following form to gauge students' skill levels entering the class (students have copies in the introductions of their student manuals). For each skill listed, have students rate their familiarity from 1 to 5, with five being the most familiar. Emphasize that this is not a test. Rather, it is intended to provide students with an idea of where they're starting from at the beginning of class. If a student is wholly unfamiliar with all the skills, he or she might not be ready for the class. A student who seems to understand all of the skills, on the other hand, might need to move on to the next course in the series.

Skill	1	2	3	4	5
Identifying the desktop components of Windows 7					
Using the Start menu and taskbar					
Using thumbnails, Aero Peek, Flip, and Flip 3-D to view open programs and files and switch between them					
Using Aero Snap and Aero Shake to manage windows and optimize your desktop for a particular task					
Using the new keyboard shortcuts for managing and arranging windows					
Customizing the Start menu, taskbar, and notification area					
Using Jump Lists to access frequently used items					
Adding and removing items on a Jump List					
Adding, modifying, and removing gadgets					
Creating and deleting libraries					
Adding folders to a library					
Removing folders from a library					
Changing the default save location for a library					
Customizing Windows Explorer					
Viewing and editing file metadata					
Searching for content					
Saving searches					
Managing devices and installing a local printer					
Backing up files					
Restoring files from a backup					
Securing your data by using BitLocker To Go					

Skill	1	2	3	4	5
Troubleshooting system and application problems					
Making older programs compatible with Windows 7					
Recording and reporting problem steps					
Using the SmartScreen Filter					
Configuring security zones in Internet Explorer					
Managing your browsing data in Internet Explorer					
Starting an InPrivate Browsing session					

Topic C: Classroom setup

All our courses assume that each student has a personal computer to use during the class. Our hands-on approach to learning requires that they do. This topic gives information on how to set up the classroom to teach this course. It includes minimum requirements for the students' personal computers, setup information for the first time you teach the class, and setup information for each time that you teach after the first time you set up the classroom.

Hardware requirements

Each student's personal computer should have:

- 1 GHz or faster 32- or 64-bit processor
- At least 1 GB of RAM (for 32-bit version), or 2 GB of RAM (for 64-bit version)
- At least 16 GB of available disk space for 32-bit version, or at least 20 GB of available disk space for 64-bit version (40 GB or more is recommended)
- An XGA monitor set to a minimum resolution of 1024×768
- A video adapter card compatible with DirectX 9 or newer, with at least 64 MB of video memory
- A sound card with a working system speaker (peripheral speakers are also acceptable)
- A keyboard and a mouse
- A DVD drive for installing Windows 7
- A writable DVD drive and a blank, writable DVD, preferably formatted (These are needed for activity A-1 in the unit titled "File protection and troubleshooting." You could also use a network location for backup storage instead of individual blank DVDs.)
- Empty USB memory devices, preferably as small as 256 MB (These are needed for activity A-3 in the unit titled "File protection and troubleshooting." If multiple devices are not obtainable, be prepared to conduct an instructor demonstration for this activity.)
- Optional: A network storage device for students to use instead of individual DVDs for creating backups in activities A-1 and A-2 in the unit titled "File protection and troubleshooting."

Note: The hardware you use will determine the Windows 7 features that are enabled. For example, the default user interface theme is determined by the type of graphics card in the computer. Therefore, we strongly recommend that you standardize the equipment in your classroom. Furthermore, we recommend that you key through the course before teaching it and be prepared to help students through sections where keystrokes and screenshots might vary from those in this manual.

Software requirements

You will also need the following software:

- Windows 7 Professional, Windows 7 Ultimate, or Windows 7 Enterprise. You'll need a copy of the installation DVD for each student computer.

  Note: This course was tested using Windows 7 Ultimate. The Ultimate edition or Enterprise edition is required to complete activity B-3 in the unit titled "File protection and troubleshooting."

Network requirements

The following network components and connectivity are also required for this course:

- Internet access, for the following purposes:
  - Downloading the latest critical updates and service packs from www.windowsupdate.com
  - Completing some of the activities
  - Downloading the Student Data files from www.axzopress.com (if necessary)

First-time setup instructions

The first time you teach this course, you will need to perform the following steps to set up each student computer:

1. Install Windows 7 on an NTFS partition according to the software manufacturer's instructions, following these additional detail steps:
   a. If prompted, click the button specifying to go online and get the latest updates.
   b. In the Set Up Windows dialog box, in the "Type a user name" box, type **Admin**.
   c. In the "Type a computer name" box, type **Computer01**. (You'll name each subsequent PC Computer02, Computer03, and so on.) Students will need to know the names of their computers, so you might want to put a card with this information on it next to each computer.
   d. Click Next. In the Type a password box, type **!pass**. In the Password Hint box, type **Exclamation abbreviation**.

      Note: This password is referenced in this course, so it's important that you enter this password.
   e. Click Next. Enter your Windows 7 product key, and click Next.
   f. On the "Help protect your computer and improve Windows automatically" screen, click "Use recommended settings."
   g. Click Next. From the Time zone list, select your time zone, and verify the accuracy of the current time. Edit the time if necessary.
   h. Click Next. On the Windows networking screen, select Work. Windows completes the setup and displays the desktop.
2. Open the Control Panel. Under User Accounts and Family Safety, click "Add or remove user accounts." Then click "Create a new account."
3. Create a standard user account named **User##** where ## is the computer number. For example, on Computer01 you would create a user account named User01.
4. If you don't have the data CD that came with this manual, download the Student Data files for the course. You can download the data directly to student machines, to a central location on your own network, or to a disk.
   a. Connect to www.axzopress.com.
   b. Under Downloads, click Instructor-Led Training.
   c. Browse the subject categories to locate your course. Then click the course title to display a list of available downloads. (You can also access these downloads through our Catalog listings.)
   d. Click the link(s) for downloading the Student Data files, and follow the instructions that appear on your screen.

5 Download and install the latest free version of Ad-Aware from www.lavasoftusa.com. Do not install Google Chrome or other applications. Do not restart or run AdAware.
6 Close all windows and log off.
7 Log on as **User##**.
8 Move the Student Data folder from C:\ to the My Documents folder of each student's user account.
9 Start Internet Explorer. In the Setup window, click Next. Select "No, don't turn on" and click Next. Select "Use express settings" and click Finish. Close Internet Explorer.

   Note: Future versions of Internet Explorer might require different basic setup steps. If you prefer, you can guide students through these steps the first time they start Internet Explorer.
10 Log off.

Note: Set up an instructor computer that you can use for demonstrations and for projecting the accompanying PowerPoint slides.

Setup instructions for every class

Because so many system settings are modified during class, every time you teach this course, you will need to perform the steps in the "First-time setup instructions" section of this document.

CertBlaster pre- and post-assessment software

CertBlaster pre- and post-assessment software is available for this course. To download and install this free software, students should complete the following steps:

1 Go to www.axzopress.com.
2 Under Downloads, click CertBlaster.
3 Click the link for Windows 7.
4 Save the .EXE file to a folder on your hard drive. (**Note:** If you skip this step, the CertBlaster software will not install correctly.)
5 Click Start and choose Run.
6 Click Browse and then navigate to the folder that contains the .EXE file.
7 Select the .EXE file and click Open.
8 Click OK and follow the on-screen instructions. When prompted for the password, enter **c_Win7**.

Topic D: Support

Your success is our primary concern. If you need help setting up this class or teaching a particular unit, topic, or activity, please don't hesitate to get in touch with us.

Contacting us

Please contact us through our Web site, www.axzopress.com. You will need to provide the name of the course, and be as specific as possible about the kind of help you need.

Instructor's tools

Our Web site provides several instructor's tools for each course, including course outlines and answers to frequently asked questions. To download these files, go to www.axzopress.com. Then, under Downloads, click Instructor-Led Training and browse our subject categories.

Unit 1

The Windows 7 environment

Unit time: 30 minutes

Complete this unit, and you'll know how to:

A Identify the desktop components.

B Use the Start menu and taskbar.

C Switch between open files and programs, and move and resize windows.

Topic A: The Windows 7 desktop

Explanation

Windows 7 introduces several new features and enhancements. You'll start exploring these features by identifying the desktop components.

Desktop components

After you log on to the computer, the Windows desktop is displayed. The desktop is the primary environment, and it provides access to all of your programs and files. The default desktop image is blue, but you can select an image as your desktop background. Exhibit 1-1 shows a custom desktop background and various desktop components.

This is not the default background image.

Tell students they will learn about gadgets later in the course.

Exhibit 1-1: Windows 7 desktop components

The following table describes the major desktop components.

Component	Description
Background	The background is a color or image that fills the screen and extends behind the other desktop elements. You can customize your desktop background.
Icons and shortcuts	An *icon* is a small pictorial representation of a program, command, or data file on the computer. Double-clicking a desktop icon opens it. By default, the desktop contains an icon for the Recycle Bin. A *shortcut* is an icon that is a link to a file, folder, or program that resides elsewhere on the computer (not on the desktop). A shortcut has a small curved arrow in the corner of the icon.
Gadgets	Gadgets are small programs that usually perform a single, simple function. Examples include a clock, a calculator, news feeds, and small games and slide shows.
Taskbar	The taskbar is a rectangular bar that contains the Start button, pinned icons and open-program icons (next to the Start button), the notification area (where the clock is located), and the Show Desktop button.
Start button	You can use the Start button to open applications and to access any file, resource, or feature on the computer.
Pinned icons	These are icons for commonly used programs, pinned to the taskbar for easy access. You can open these items with a single click.
Notification area	Also called the system tray, this area contains the date and time, the volume control, and any icons showing the status of background programs.
Show Desktop	This is a small rectangular button at the far end of the taskbar. Pointing to the Show Desktop button will make open windows look transparent. Clicking the button will minimize all windows so you can see the entire desktop.

Do it!

A-1: Identifying desktop components

The logon screen should be displayed.

Tell students they will use this account throughout the course.

Help students locate this button if necessary.

Here's how	Here's why
1 Observe the logon screen	Note the available user accounts.
2 Click **User##**	(Where ## is your computer number.) Your user name was created during the installation and setup of Windows 7.
3 Locate the Recycle Bin	 (On the desktop.) The Recycle Bin is your computer's trash bin. Deleted items are stored here until you empty the trash. If you change your mind and want to keep some items you have deleted, you can retrieve them from the Recycle Bin before you empty it.
4 Identify the taskbar	(At the bottom of the screen.) The taskbar contains the Start button and the notification area. Pinned icons for frequently used programs appear to the right of the Start button. You can customize your pinned programs.
5 Locate the Start button	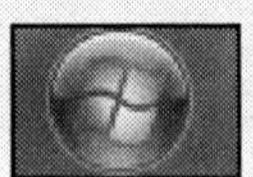 (On the taskbar.) You can use this button to start just about any activity on your computer, including opening applications, getting help, configuring your computer, searching for items on your computer, and shutting down your computer.
6 Locate the pinned icons	 (To the right of the Start button.) These represent commonly used programs. You decide what programs go here. By default, there are pinned icons for Internet Explorer, Windows Explorer, and Windows Media Player.
7 Identify the notification area	(The right end of the taskbar.) It contains a clock that displays the current time, and it might contain icons for programs or other options on your computer. Any system alerts, reminders, or warnings will be displayed here.
8 Locate the Show Desktop button	(At the far right edge of the taskbar.) You can click this button to minimize all open windows.

Topic B: The Start menu and taskbar

Explanation

The taskbar contains the Start button, program icons, and the notification area. It has changed in both behavior and appearance from previous versions of Windows. You can still use the Start button to open applications and to access any resource on the computer. To the right of the Start button on the taskbar are "pinned" icons, used to launch your most frequently used programs. Pinned icons replace the Quick Launch bar in previous versions of Windows.

The Start menu

You can use the Start menu, shown in Exhibit 1-2, to open applications, configure your computer, search for files on your computer, shut down your computer, and perform other tasks. To open the Start menu, you can click the Start button, press the Windows key, or press Ctrl+Esc.

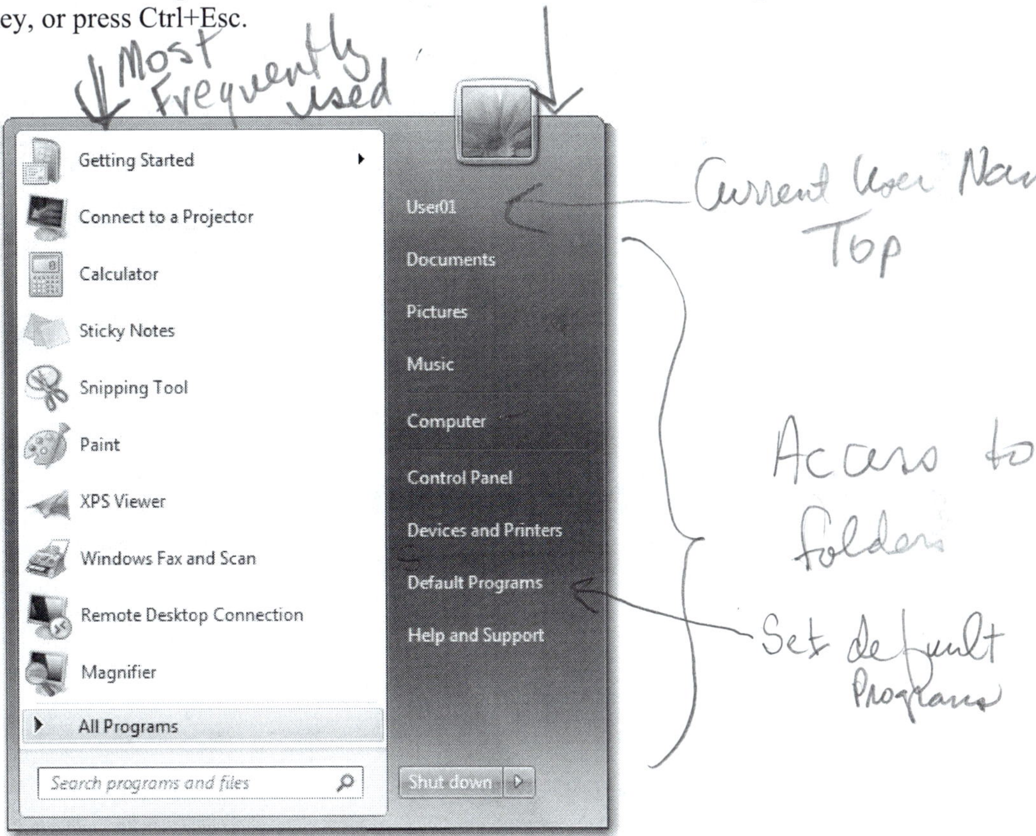

Exhibit 1-2: The Start menu

The Start menu is divided into two panes. The left pane contains the most frequently used programs (when you first install Windows, default programs are listed). You can click All Programs to navigate to all of your programs. At the bottom of the Start menu, there's a text box you can use to search for files and folders on your computer.

The current user account name and icon appear at the top of the menu's right pane. The options in the right pane provide access to folders, including Documents, Pictures, and Music. You can also open the Control Panel and Help and Support.

Taskbar icons

Students will learn more about pinning program icons later in the course.

When you start Windows 7, you'll see three icons "pinned" to the taskbar by default: Internet Explorer, Windows Explorer, and Windows Media Player. *Pinned icons* stay on the taskbar and open your most frequently used programs. Click once on a pinned taskbar icon to start a program. When you open a program that has a pinned taskbar icon, its icon is highlighted but a new icon does not appear on the taskbar. This differs from previous Windows versions. Before, starting a program by clicking an icon on the Quick Launch bar would add another taskbar icon.

The Windows 7 taskbar is program-oriented rather than window-oriented. If you open multiple instances of a program or open multiple documents in the same program (e.g., three WordPad documents), only one icon will be displayed. It will look as if several icons have been stacked atop each other, as shown in Exhibit 1-3, with each layer in the stack representing an open document or an instance of the program. Also, window labels are no longer displayed on taskbar icons, thus conserving more space on the taskbar.

Icons for open programs look the same whether they are pinned or not—you can't tell if an open icon is pinned by looking at it. The icon for the active program appears lighter than the other icons.

Unpinned icons appear on the taskbar in the order in which you open the programs. You can drag any of the program icons—even the pinned ones—to change their order.

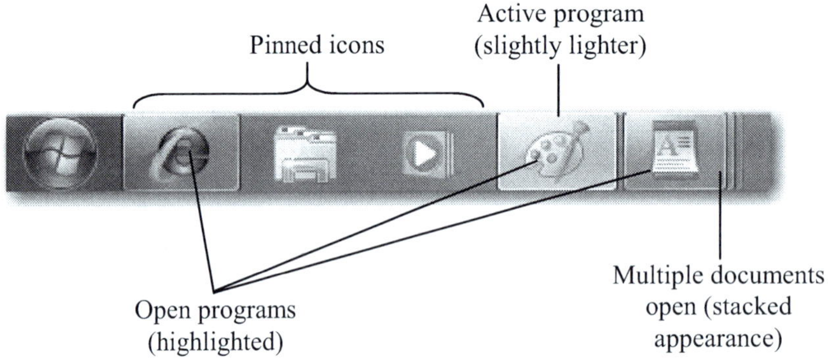

Exhibit 1-3: Icons on the taskbar

Do it!

B-1: Exploring the Start menu and taskbar

Here's how	Here's why
1 Point to [Start button]	This is the Start button. A ToolTip appears after a moment.
2 Click the Start button	To display the Start menu, which is divided into two panes.

Tell students that the items on the Start menu will vary depending on what's installed on the computer and which programs are used most often.

Instructor notes	Step	Result
	3 Observe the All Programs command	▸ **All Programs** The triangle indicates that this command opens a submenu.
	4 Click **All Programs**	The All Programs submenu opens in the left pane, displaying folders and applications.
Tell students that they'll open various programs so they can switch between them in the next activity.	Click **Accessories**	To expand Accessories and display the items it contains.
	5 Click **WordPad**	To open the WordPad application.
	Observe the taskbar	An icon for WordPad has appeared.
Point out that WordPad has been added to the Start menu.	6 Click **Start**	WordPad has been added to the Start menu. As you use Windows 7 over time, your most frequently used programs will be displayed in the Start menu.
	Choose **Calculator**	To open the Calculator application.
	Observe the taskbar	The taskbar icon for the Calculator appears highlighted because it's the active program.
	7 Open **Paint**	Click Start and choose All Programs, Accessories, Paint.
	8 Click the icon for Internet Explorer	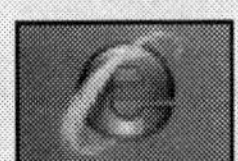 (On the taskbar.) To open Internet Explorer. The default home page, MSN.com, opens in the browser. Windows does not add a new icon to the taskbar; instead, it highlights the pinned icon.
	9 In the browser, click the blank tab, as shown	 To open a new browser tab. The taskbar icon for Internet Explorer now has a stacked appearance.
Tell students that they will explore switching between these items in the next activity. Be sure they leave all windows open.	10 In the Address bar, type **bing.com** and press ENTER	To open the bing.com site. In the next topic, you'll use different methods to switch between multiple windows.

Topic C: Window management

Explanation

When you're working with several open files and programs, you'll often need to switch back and forth between those open items. As you work, you'll also need to resize windows or move them around to optimize your desktop for a particular task.

Switching between open files and programs

The traditional Windows methods for switching among open programs and files are still available. Some features have been enhanced, and some new window management methods have been introduced. In Windows 7, you can use taskbar thumbnails, Flip, and Flip 3-D to quickly switch among your open files and programs.

Live thumbnails and Aero Peek

Aero Peek is a new usability enhancement.

Pointing to the taskbar icon of a running program opens a "live thumbnail"—a small image—of that program window, even if it's hidden from view on the desktop. A live thumbnail reflects what's happening in the window, so if a video is playing or a progress bar is in motion, you'll see these things moving in the thumbnail.

You can interact with window thumbnails. You can close a window from its thumbnail, and you can "peek" at a window by pointing to its thumbnail. As shown in Exhibit 1-4, pointing to a thumbnail brings that window to the forefront and makes all other windows transparent, thereby giving you a "peek" at the window at full size—without actually switching to the window. (To switch to a window on the desktop, you can click its thumbnail.) This feature, called *Aero Peek*, is useful when you're working with several windows.

If you have multiple windows open and you want a quick look at the items on your desktop, you can hold down the Windows key and press Spacebar. All windows will become transparent. Release the Windows key to return the windows to their previous states.

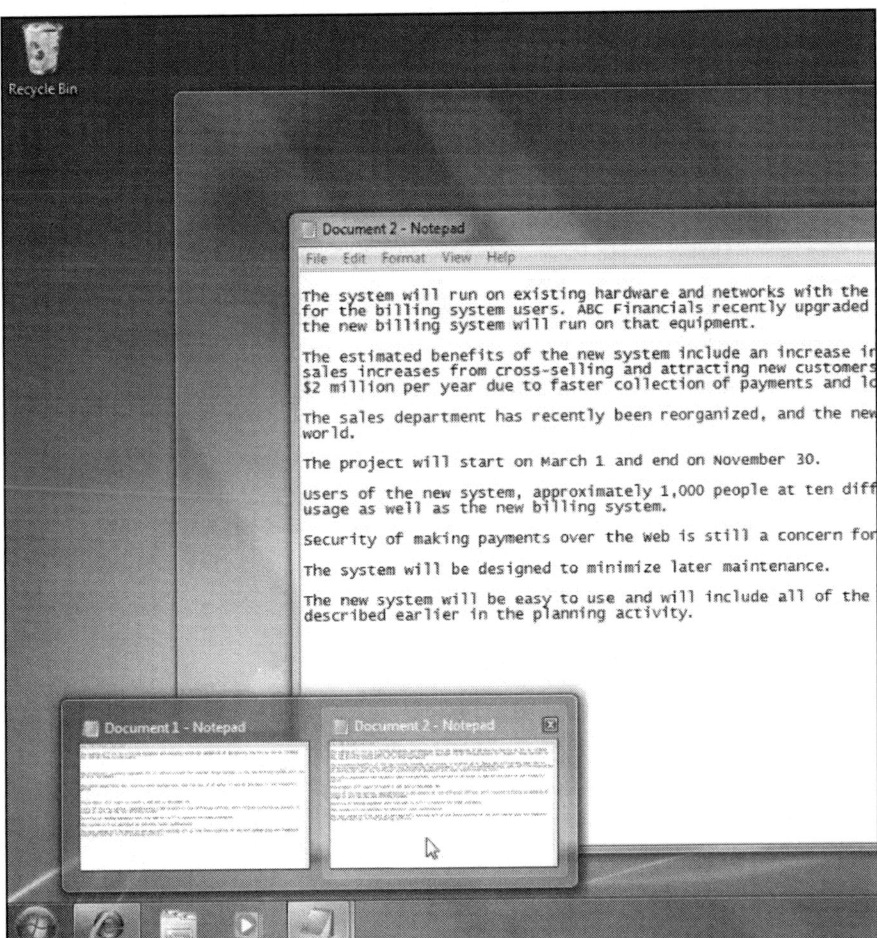

Exhibit 1-4: Thumbnails show you multiple open files at a glance

Flip

You can also flip through open applications and the desktop by pressing Alt+Tab. This key combination displays thumbnails of all open programs, as shown in Exhibit 1-5. You can scroll through them by holding down the Alt key and pressing the Tab key.

Exhibit 1-5: Use Alt+Tab to "flip" between open items

Flip 3-D

You can hold down the Windows key and press Tab to flip through 3-D versions of your open windows, as shown in Exhibit 1-6.

Exhibit 1-6: Use the Windows key and Tab to flip between open items in 3-D

The Show Desktop button

The Show Desktop icon in previous versions of Windows has been replaced by a small rectangle at the far right end of the taskbar. This is the Show Desktop button. If you point to it, all open windows become transparent, and you can see the desktop. Click it, and all windows are minimized.

Aero effects and system resources

If your system does not have sufficient graphics resources, some of the interface features, like the Aero transparency effects, will not be available. You can also turn these features off manually.

Do it!

C-1: Switching between windows

	Here's how	Here's why
Internet Explorer is active.	1 Verify that Internet Explorer is active	
	2 On the taskbar, point to the Internet Explorer icon	Thumbnails for both browser tabs appear.
	Point to one of the thumbnails	That browser tab becomes active, and all other open windows on the desktop become transparent.
Tell students this is called Aero Peek.	Point to the other thumbnail	To quickly "peek" at the other browser tab.
	3 Point to the Calculator icon	(On the taskbar.) A thumbnail of the calculator appears.
	Point to the thumbnail	All other windows become transparent, showing only the calculator on the desktop.
	4 Point to the WordPad icon	
	Point to the WordPad thumbnail	To get a peek at the WordPad window and make all other windows transparent.
	5 Hold down ALT	
Tell students this feature is called Flip.	Press TAB several times	All windows appear as thumbnails in a row across the screen; a different window is highlighted each time you press Tab.
	Pause when the desktop thumbnail is selected	All other windows become transparent.
If a different window is selected when students release Alt, that window will be displayed above the other windows.	Release ALT	To switch to the desktop. This minimizes all windows.
	6 Click the Show Desktop button	(The rectangle at the far right end of the taskbar.) To show all windows again. This is a toggle button; if the desktop is already shown, clicking it shows the active windows.
	7 Hold down the Windows key	If your keyboard has one.
Tell students this feature is called Flip 3-D.	Press TAB several times	To flip through the windows in 3-D, even if some or all windows are minimized.
	Pause when Internet Explorer is at the front of the 3-D list	While still holding down the Windows key.
If their pointer is still over the Show Desktop button, all windows will appear transparent.	Release the Windows key	To switch to Internet Explorer.

8	Right-click the Internet Explorer icon and choose **Close Window**	You'll close this program. A dialog box asks if you want to close all tabs or just the current one.
	Click **Close all tabs**	To close Internet Explorer.
9	Point to the Show Desktop button	All windows become transparent.
	Move the pointer away	The windows are displayed again.
10	Click the Show Desktop button	All windows are minimized.
	Click it again	All windows are restored.
11	Hold down the Windows key and press SPACEBAR	To quickly peek at the desktop. This shortcut is useful if you have multiple windows open and you want to get a quick look at desktop items.
	Release the Windows key	

Moving and resizing windows

Explanation

All of the traditional methods you have used in the past to move and resize windows are still available. For example, to move a window, you can drag its title bar. To resize a window, you can drag its edges or corners in the direction you want. To maximize a window, you double-click its title bar; double-click it again to restore the window to its former size. In addition to keeping these standard methods, Windows 7 introduces Aero Snap and Aero Shake.

Aero Snap

Aero Snap is a new usability enhancement that helps you to precisely arrange your windows on the desktop. Here's how Aero Snap works:

- To maximize a window, drag its title bar up until the pointer hits the top of the screen. To restore the window to its former size, drag it down.

  You can also hold down the Windows key and press the Up Arrow key.
- To resize a window so it takes up half of the desktop, drag the window's title bar to the left or right until the pointer hits the edge of the screen. A quick way to compare two windows is to drag one to the left side and one to the right. To restore the window to its former size, drag it away from the edge of the screen.

  You can also hold down the Windows key and press the Left or Right Arrow key to snap a window to one side.
- To resize a window so it uses the full height of the screen, but without changing the width, drag the window's bottom edge down to the bottom of the screen.

  You can also hold down the Windows and Shift keys and press Up Arrow to vertically maximize a window.

Aero Shake

Tell students that both Aero Snap and Aero Shake are new in Windows 7.

Another new usability feature in Windows 7 is called *Aero Shake*. If you have multiple windows open and you want to quickly minimize all but one window, you can "shake" the desired window by quickly dragging the title bar back and forth. Shake the window again to restore all the other windows.

You can also use a keyboard shortcut as an alternative to shaking a window. Hold down the Windows key and press Home to minimize all windows except the active window.

Do it!

C-2: Moving and resizing windows

⚠ *Ensure that the window is not maximized. Otherwise, students will not be able to resize it. Also, ensure that none of the window edges are beyond the screen's display area.*

Point out that this is a standard window resizing method—all of the old window management methods still apply in Windows 7.

Here's how	Here's why
1 Activate WordPad	Click its taskbar icon.
2 From the title bar, drag the window as far left as you can	When the pointer reaches the left side of the screen, the window "snaps" to the left side and occupies half of the screen.
3 Activate Paint	Click its taskbar icon.
Drag the window as far right as you can	When the pointer reaches the right side of the screen, the window "snaps" to the right side, filling up the other half of the screen. You can use this method to quickly view documents or other items side by side.
4 Activate Calculator	
Point to the title bar, and then drag it back and forth quickly	To minimize all other windows. This method, called Aero Shake, allows you to quickly focus on one window when multiple windows are open.
Shake the Calculator again	To restore the other windows to their previous states.
5 Hold down the Windows key	
Press (HOME)	To minimize all windows except the active window. This is a keyboard alternative to Aero Shake.
Press (HOME) again	To restore all windows.
Release the Windows key	
6 Point to the right edge of the window on the left	The pointer changes to a two-sided arrow, indicating that you can resize the window in either direction.
Drag to the right	To resize the window.
7 From the title bar, drag the other window downward	To move the window down on the screen.
8 Drag that same window as far to the top as you can	To maximize the window. This method is an alternative to clicking the Maximize button or double-clicking the title bar.
From the title bar, drag the maximized window downward	To restore the window to its previous size.

9	Click the Show Desktop button	To minimize all windows.
	Click it again	To restore all open windows.
10	Close all open windows	

Unit summary: The Windows 7 environment

Topic A In this topic, you logged on to Windows 7 and identified the various **desktop components**. The desktop is the primary environment and provides access to all of your programs and files.

Topic B In this topic, you explored the new look and features of the **taskbar** and **Start menu**.

Topic C In this topic, you learned how to use **thumbnails**, **Aero Peek**, **Flip**, and **Flip 3-D** to access specific windows when you're working with multiple programs and files. You learned how to use **Aero Snap** and **Aero Shake**, two new features for resizing, moving, and minimizing windows. You also learned several keyboard shortcuts for managing and arranging windows.

Review questions

1 What are pinned icons?

Icons for commonly used programs, pinned to the taskbar for easy access. You can open these items with a single click.

2 How can you navigate to all of your programs from the Start menu?

Click Start and choose All Programs.

3 How can you search for anything on your PC right from the Start menu?

Click Start, type your search text, and press Enter.

4 Where is the new Show Desktop button located?

The Show Desktop button is at the far right end of the taskbar. Click it to minimize all windows. Click it again to restore all windows to their previous states.

5 What happens if you hold down the Windows key and press Tab?

You will cycle through all open windows in 3-D. To activate a particular window, release the Windows key when the thumbnail for that window is at the front of the list.

6 How might you use the Aero Snap feature?

Answers may vary. This new window arrangement method provides a quick way to compare two windows side by side, for example.

7 What is the keyboard shortcut to minimize all windows except the active window?

Hold down the Windows key and press Home.

8 What is the keyboard shortcut to quickly peek at the desktop?

Hold down the Windows key and press Spacebar.

9 What is the keyboard shortcut to snap a window to the left half of the screen?

Hold down the Windows key and press the Left Arrow key.

Independent practice activity

In this activity, you'll open some programs and use a few methods to switch between them and organize them on the desktop.

1 Open Paint, Calculator, and Internet Explorer.

2 Open two instances of WordPad.

3 Use Alt+Tab to flip between the programs and activate Paint.

4 Use Flip 3-D to switch to Internet Explorer.

5 On the taskbar, point to the WordPad icon.

6 Activate one of the WordPad windows. Snap it to the right side of the screen.

7 Close all open windows.

Unit 2

Customizing the environment

Unit time: 30 minutes

Complete this unit, and you'll know how to:

A Customize the taskbar, Start menu, and notification area, and use Jump Lists.

B Use gadgets.

Topic A: Customizing the taskbar and Start menu

Explanation

You can add or remove program icons on both the taskbar and the Start menu. You can also rearrange program icons to customize your environment and work more efficiently.

Pinning programs to the taskbar and Start menu

One way you can customize your Windows environment is to change the program icons on the taskbar and Start menu to the programs that you use most frequently. When you pin an icon to the taskbar or Start menu, it will remain there until you unpin it.

To pin a program icon to the taskbar, do either of the following:

- Drag a program shortcut from the Start menu, the desktop, or Windows Explorer onto the taskbar.
- Right-click a program shortcut on the Start menu, in Windows Explorer, or on the desktop, and choose Pin to Taskbar.

By default, the left pane of the Start menu contains a few program shortcuts. As you use Windows, these programs will change to reflect recently and frequently used programs. If you want a program to stay on the Start menu no matter how often you use it, you can pin it there—just right-click the shortcut and choose Pin to Start Menu. The shortcut moves to the top section of the Start menu, above a faint dividing line. As with taskbar icons, you can rearrange these pinned icons by dragging them.

You can also pin program icons to the Start menu from other locations, as follows:

- Drag a program shortcut from the desktop or Windows Explorer onto the Start button, wait a moment for the Start menu to open, and then drop the shortcut in the desired location on the menu.
- Right-click a program shortcut on the desktop or in Windows Explorer, and choose Pin to Start Menu.

Do it!

A-1: Pinning icons for your frequently used programs

Here's how	Here's why
1 Click **Start** and choose **All Programs**, **Accessories**	
2 Right-click **WordPad** and choose **Pin to Start Menu**	
3 Click **Back**	(At the bottom of the Start menu.) To return to the main Start menu. WordPad is now at the top of the menu, over a light dividing line. It will remain here unless you unpin it. The programs listed below the dividing line will change over time as you use different programs.
4 Pin Notepad to the Start menu	
5 Pin Calculator to the Start menu	
6 Drag Calculator to the top of the list, as shown	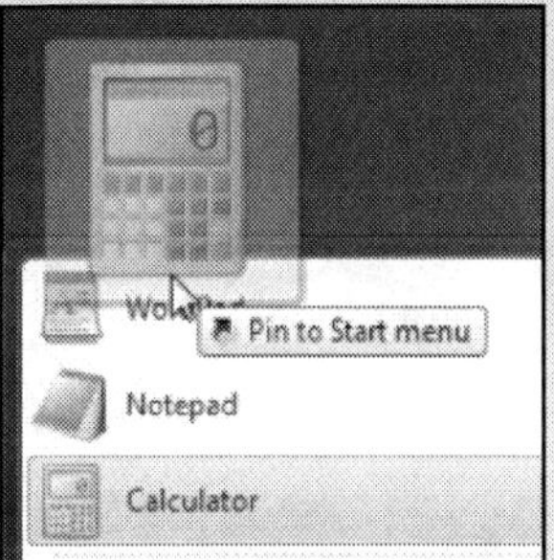 To rearrange the pinned Start menu icons. You can rearrange any Start menu or taskbar items as needed.
7 Right-click **WordPad** and choose **Pin to Taskbar**	A new icon appears on the taskbar. It will remain there until you unpin it.

Removing program shortcuts

Explanation

You can remove shortcuts and taskbar icons without affecting the actual application, file, or folder that they refer to. Only the shortcut is deleted.

You can remove both pinned and automatically added icons from the Start menu and taskbar. You might remove pinned items if you no longer use them regularly. Generally, you won't need to remove the items that have been added automatically because as you use new programs, old items are removed automatically.

To remove a taskbar icon:

1. Right-click the icon.
2. Choose "Unpin this program from taskbar."

To remove a pinned menu item:

1. Open the Start menu.
2. Right-click the item and choose Unpin from Start Menu.

To remove an unpinned item from the Start menu:

1. Open the Start menu.
2. Right-click the item and choose "Remove from this list."

Do it!

A-2: Removing Start menu shortcuts and taskbar icons

Here's how	Here's why
1 Open the Start menu	You'll delete a shortcut and unpin another.
2 Right-click **Calculator**	
Choose **Unpin from Start Menu**	To unpin the shortcut.
3 Right-click **Windows Media Center**	
Choose **Remove from this list**	
4 On the taskbar, right-click the Windows Media Player icon	
Choose **Unpin this program from taskbar**	The program icon is removed.

Customizing the Start menu, taskbar, and notification area

Explanation

Aside from adding and removing program icons, you can customize the taskbar and Start menu in other ways. For example, you can affix the taskbar to any edge of the screen, or use small icons so that the taskbar takes up less space. Right-click an empty area of the taskbar and choose Properties, and then make the desired changes.

You can change several properties of the Start menu by using the Customize Start Menu dialog box, shown in Exhibit 2-1. For example, you can change the number of programs shown on the recent-programs list, or you can choose not to display recently opened documents. You can also control which items are displayed on the right side of the Start menu and how they are displayed.

To open the Customize Start Menu dialog box, right-click the Start button, choose Properties, and click Customize on the Start Menu tab. Make your changes, and click OK.

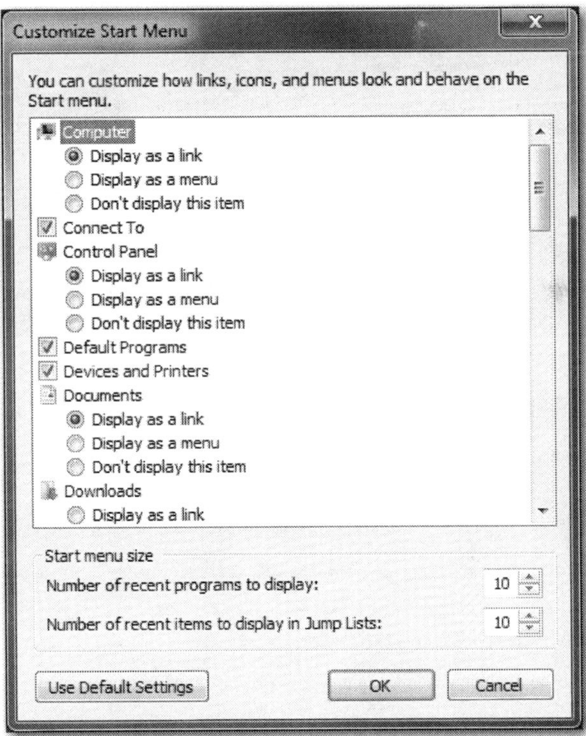

Exhibit 2-1: Options for customizing the Start menu

Customizing the notification area

In previous versions of Windows, the notification area (also called the system tray) could become cluttered as new programs and utilities were installed. Windows 7 gives you better control over system notifications and icons. You can choose which icons are displayed in the notification area, and you can hide icons and show only notifications.

To customize the notification area, right-click an empty area of the taskbar and choose Properties. Then click Customize to open the Notification Area Icons window, shown in Exhibit 2-2. Use the drop-down lists next to each icon to customize the settings, and click OK.

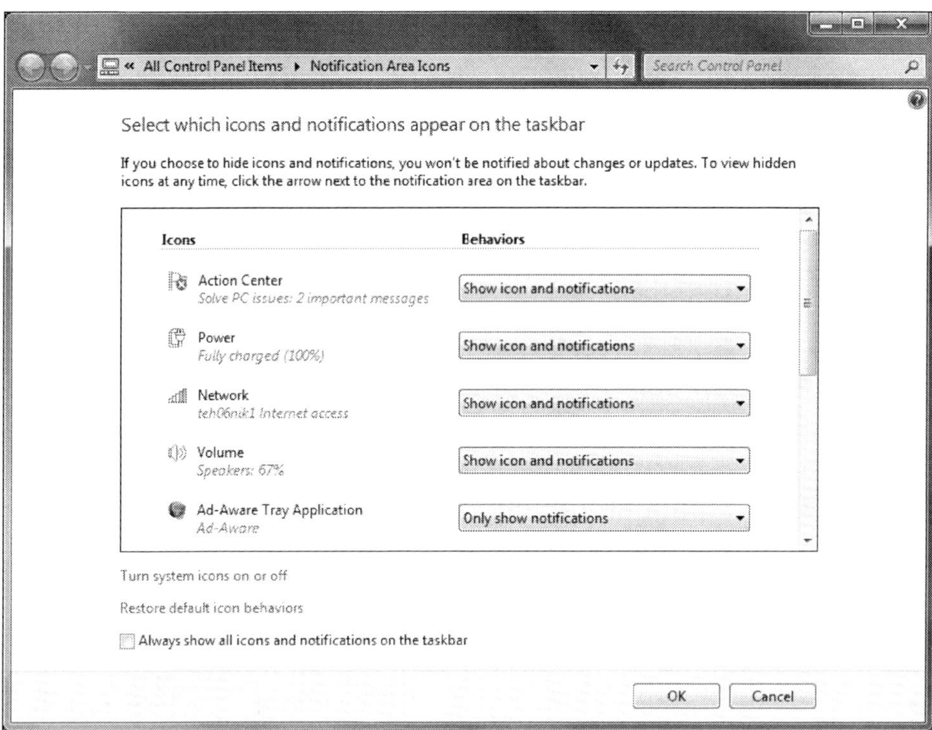

Exhibit 2-2: Customizing the notification area of the taskbar

Do it!

A-3: Customizing Start menu and taskbar properties

Here's how	Here's why
1 Right-click a blank area of the taskbar and choose **Properties**	To open the Taskbar and Start Menu Properties dialog box.
2 Activate the Start Menu tab	
Observe the options under Privacy	You can set Windows so it does not store or show recently opened items.
3 Click **Customize**	To open the Customize Start Menu dialog box.
Briefly scan the customization options	(Scroll down to see them all.) You can also change the number of recent programs and documents that are displayed.

4 Change the "Number of recent programs to display" to **5**	(At the bottom of the dialog box.) Click the arrow button, or just select the number and type 5.
5 Click **OK**	To close the Customize Start Menu dialog box and return to the Properties dialog box.
6 Click **Apply**	To apply the changes without closing the dialog box.
7 Click **Start** and observe the menu	Only five programs are now listed, not including the pinned programs.
Click **Start**	To close the Start menu and return to the Properties dialog box.
8 Click **Customize**	
Click **Use Default Settings**	Notice that the number of recent programs changes back to 10. You can always return the Start menu to its default properties with a single click.
Click **OK**	
9 Observe the notification area of the taskbar	A volume icon is among the default icons.
10 Activate the Taskbar tab	(In the Taskbar and Start Menu Properties dialog box.) You'll remove the volume icon.
Click **Customize**	To open the Notification Area Icons window.
11 Click the button next to Volume	To display a short list. You can show the icon and notifications, hide both the icon and notifications, or show only notifications.
Select **Only show notifications**	
Click **OK**	The volume icon is no longer displayed in the notification area, but any important notifications related to it will still appear.
12 Click **OK**	To close the Taskbar and Start Menu Properties dialog box.

Jump Lists

Explanation

Windows 7 introduces *Jump Lists*, which are context menus that you can use to open recent and favorite files and folders. If you right-click a program icon on the taskbar, a shortcut menu (Jump List) opens, like the one shown in Exhibit 2-3. For example, the Jump List for Internet Explorer shows your recently opened Web sites, allowing you to open those sites directly.

You can pin items to a Jump List for fast access to files that you need to open frequently. Both the taskbar and the Start menu have Jump Lists. On the taskbar, icons for open programs and pinned icons have Jump Lists. In addition to right-clicking an icon to open its Jump List, you can also drag a program icon up toward the desktop.

Exhibit 2-3: Jump Lists provide easy access to recent and favorite files

On the Start menu, program shortcuts that have Jump Lists are indicated by a small black arrow. You can point to or click a program to open its Jump List, which expands into the right pane of the Start menu, as shown in Exhibit 2-4. A program's Jump List will contain the same items on both the Start menu and the taskbar.

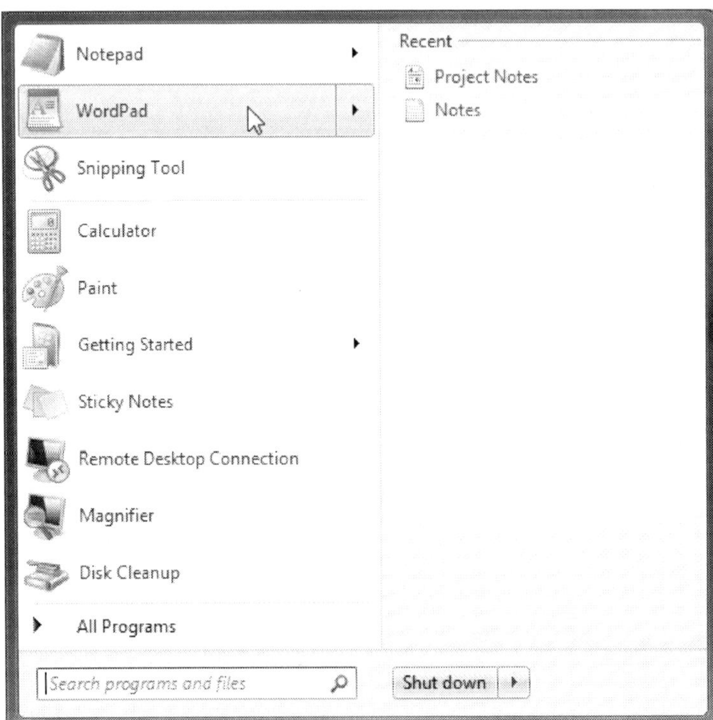

Exhibit 2-4: You can access a program's Jump List from the Start menu

Do it!

A-4: Using Jump Lists

Here's how	Here's why
1 On the taskbar, right-click the Internet Explorer icon	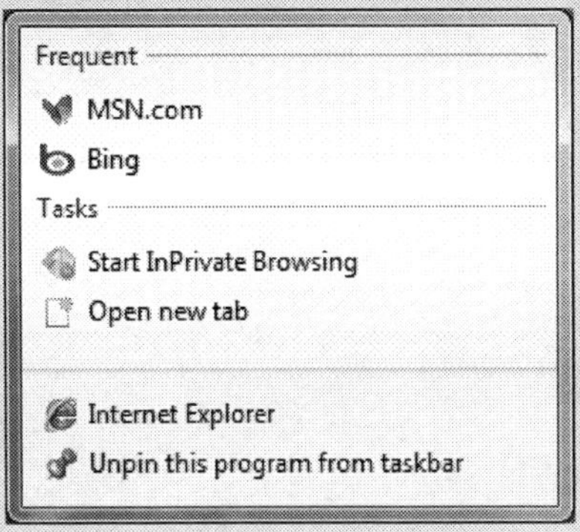 Frequent MSN.com Bing Tasks Start InPrivate Browsing Open new tab Internet Explorer Unpin this program from taskbar The Jump List for Internet Explorer opens, showing frequently visited sites and common tasks. The content in a Jump List will vary according to the program and your recent activity.
2 Click **Bing**	To go directly to the Bing search engine. You can pin your most frequently visited sites to your browser's Jump List.
3 Right-click the Internet Explorer icon again	To open the Jump List.
Right-click **Bing**	
Choose **Pin to this list**	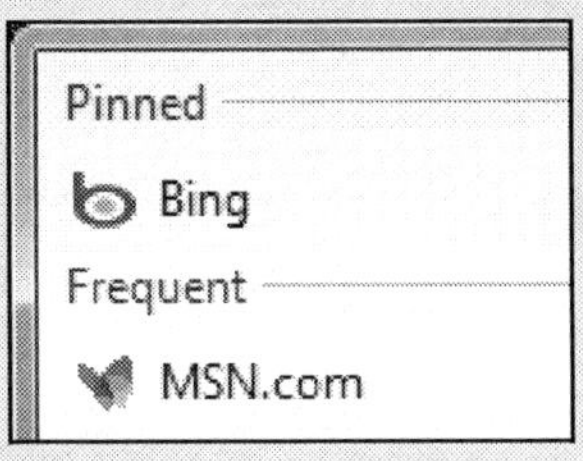 Pinned Bing Frequent MSN.com The Bing Web site now appears in the Pinned section of the Jump List. It will remain pinned to this Jump List until you unpin it.
4 Click **Start** and choose **All Programs**	
Right-click **Internet Explorer**	
Choose **Pin to Start Menu**	
5 Click **Back**	(At the bottom of the Start menu.) Internet Explorer is pinned to the Start menu.

6 In the Start menu, point to Internet Explorer	The Jump List expands into the right pane of the Start menu, and the items in the list are the same as in the taskbar Jump List.
Right-click **MSN.com**	
Choose **Remove from this list**	
7 Click **Start**	To close the Start menu.
8 Close Internet Explorer	

Topic B: Working with gadgets

Explanation

Gadgets are small, specialized programs that sit on your desktop, as shown in Exhibit 2-5. Gadgets usually perform a single, simple convenience function. Examples include a clock, a calculator, sticky notes, news feeds, and small games and slide shows.

Exhibit 2-5: Gadgets on the desktop

Adding and modifying gadgets

You add new gadgets by using the Gadget Gallery, shown in Exhibit 2-6. To open it, right-click a blank area of the desktop and choose Gadgets. Once you're in the gallery, you can right-click the gadget of your choice and choose Add, or just double-click the gadget to add it to the desktop.

The gallery starts out with just a few gadgets, but you can click the "Get more gadgets online" link to access thousands of gadgets with all kinds of functions.

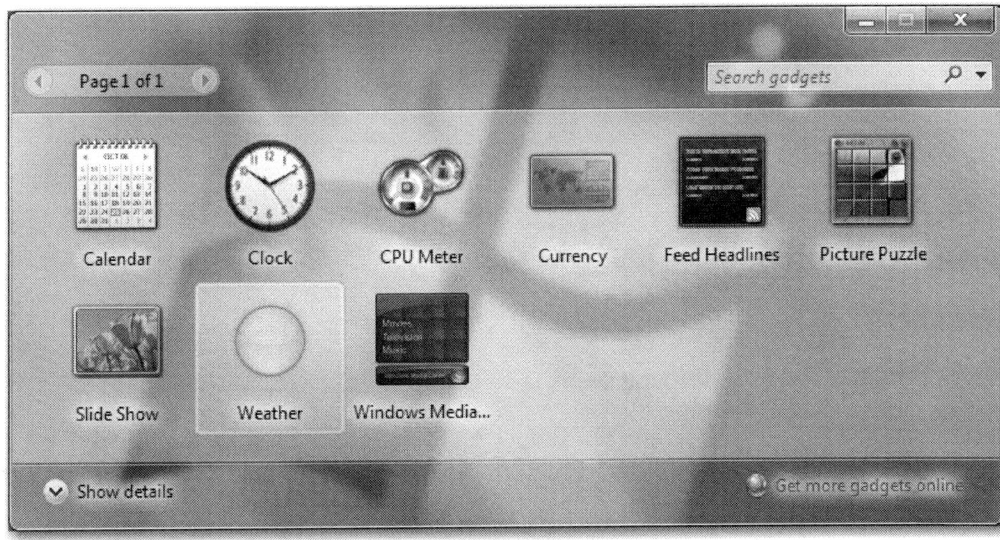

Exhibit 2-6: The Gadget Gallery

Moving gadgets

To move a gadget, click its handle and drag it on the desktop. The handle is the bottom-most control button, and it looks like a grid of dots. You can move some gadgets by dragging from anywhere on their interface, but it's usually best to drag from the handle because for some gadgets, clicking directly on them means that you want to do something else, like write a reminder note or open a news article.

Gadget options and settings

Many gadgets have properties that you can set. For example, you can choose different colors for sticky notes or set the opacity of a clock. Exhibit 2-7 shows the options for the Clock gadget.

When you point to a gadget, its control buttons appear to the right of it. Click the wrench button to open the gadget's settings. You can also right-click a gadget to open a shortcut menu of commands specific to that gadget. Some gadgets have no editable options.

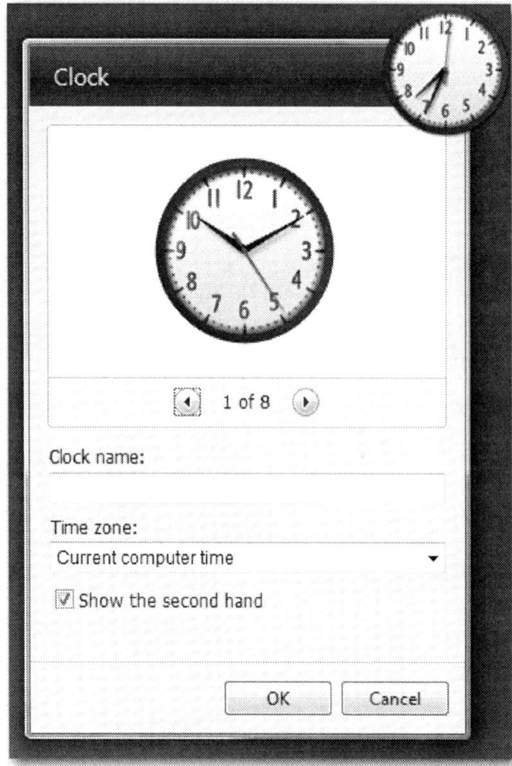

Exhibit 2-7: Changing the clock settings

Removing gadgets

To remove a gadget, point to it to display the control buttons, and then click the Close button (the X button). You can also right-click a gadget and choose Close Gadget.

Do it!

B-1: Working with gadgets

Here's how	Here's why
1 Right-click the desktop and choose **Gadgets**	To open the Gadget Gallery.
2 Double-click the Clock	The Clock gadget appears on the desktop—in the upper-right area by default.
3 Add the Calendar gadget	Double-click it. It shows today's date.
4 Close the Gadget Gallery	
5 Double-click the calendar	It changes to a monthly calendar with today's date highlighted.
Double-click today's date in the month	To go back to the original view.
6 Point to the clock gadget	When you point to a gadget, its controls appear to the right of it.
Click the wrench button, as shown	To open the clock gadget's options.
Click the right arrow	To view the next clock style.
View the different clock styles and choose the one you prefer	
Click **OK**	
7 Right-click the clock	
Choose **Opacity**, **60%**	To make the clock slightly transparent.
8 Close the calendar	Point to it and click the Close button.
9 Point to the clock	
From the handle, drag the clock downward on the desktop	The handle is the bottom control button, under the wrench.
10 Close the clock	

Unit summary: Customizing the environment

Topic A

In this topic, you learned how to customize the **taskbar**, **Start menu**, and **notification area**. You also learned how to use **Jump Lists** to access frequently used items, and you learned how to add and remove items on a Jump List.

Topic B

In this topic, you learned how to use **gadgets**. You learned how to add, move, and remove gadgets and change gadget settings.

Review questions

1 True or false? The Jump List for a program contains the same items whether you open it from the Start menu or the taskbar.

True

2 True or false? You can remove a shortcut or taskbar icon without affecting the actual application, file, or folder that it refers to.

True

3 How can you customize the notification area of the taskbar?

Right-click an empty area of the taskbar and choose Properties. Then click Customize to open the Notification Area Icons window. Make the desired changes, and click OK.

4 How do programs get added to the Start menu if you don't pin them there?

As you use programs, Windows 7 adds them to the dynamic area of the Start menu. The programs you use most often will remain in the list for your convenience.

5 On the taskbar, there are two ways that you can open a program's Jump List. One way is to right-click the program icon. What's the other method?

You can drag a program icon up toward the desktop.

Independent practice activity

In this activity, you'll customize the taskbar, pin an item to a Jump List, and add, modify, and remove a gadget.

1 Pin Calculator to the taskbar.

2 Open the Gadget Gallery. Add Slide Show to the desktop, and close the gallery.

3 Enlarge the Slide Show.

4 Open the Slide Show options. From the folder list, choose Sample Pictures. Change the interval between pictures to 5 seconds, and change the transition to Fade.

5 Close the options and watch the slide show for a few slides.

6 Remove the slideshow gadget from the desktop.

7 Unpin Calculator from the taskbar.

Unit 3

Folders, libraries, and content

Unit time: 60 minutes

Complete this unit, and you'll know how to:

A Create and manage folders and libraries.

B Customize Windows Explorer, and edit file metadata.

C Search the computer for specific content.

Topic A: Folders and libraries

Explanation

Windows 7 offers several new file and folder management features. Windows Explorer has been redesigned to improve usability and provide new ways to organize and search for data. The new libraries allow you to organize all files of a certain type in a single location for faster access and more efficient searching.

Windows Explorer

There are several ways to open Windows Explorer, and what you see will depend on the location or library you start in. For example, if you click Start and choose Computer, Windows Explorer opens at the computer level, with hard disks and other devices shown in the contents pane. If you click the Windows Explorer icon on the taskbar, you'll start with all four libraries shown in the contents pane.

There are several ways you can customize your view of your files and folders. Exhibit 3-1 shows the components of a window. In this window, the Pictures library is open, the files are in List view, and the preview pane is displayed.

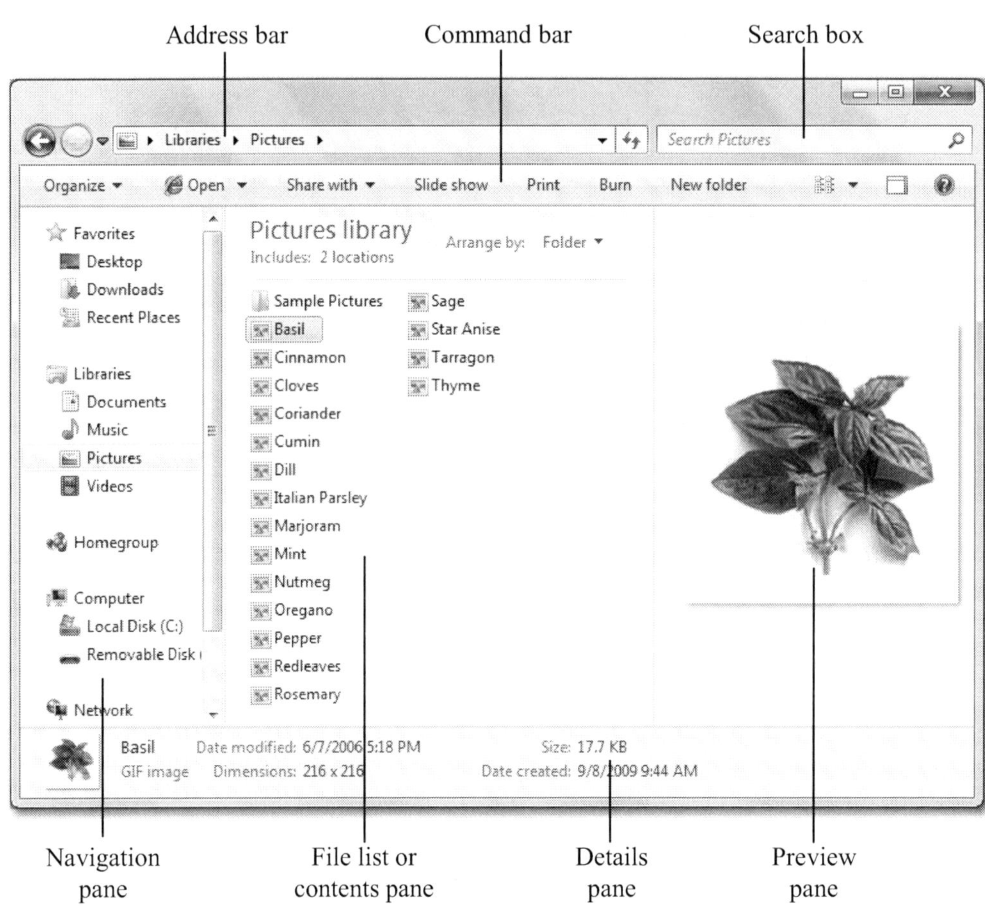

Exhibit 3-1: Windows Explorer, showing the Pictures library, with the preview pane active

These window components are described in the following table.

Component	Description
Address bar	Shows your current location in the computer's folder hierarchy. You can click an arrow next to a folder to see a list of folders beneath it.
Command bar	Contains buttons you can use to create folders, share files and folders with other users, and change how content is displayed. You can also click the Help button to get help with what you're doing. The Command bar is dynamic, which means that the commands change depending on what you're viewing.
Search box	Used to enter words or phrases to search for content containing those words or phrases.
Navigation pane	Used to move through the folder hierarchy and other locations, like libraries, removable storage devices, and network locations.
Folder list pane or contents pane	Displays drives, devices, folders, and files in the location that is selected in the navigation pane.
Details pane	Displays detailed information for the selected drive, device, folder, or file.
Preview pane	Displays the contents of the selected file. Click the "Show preview pane" button on the Command bar to display the pane, and click it again to hide it.

Do it!

A-1: Browsing folders in Windows Explorer

Tell students they will learn more about libraries in the next section.

	Here's how	Here's why
1	On the taskbar, click the Windows Explorer icon	Windows Explorer opens, showing four libraries.
2	In the navigation pane, click **Computer**	Your computer's hard drive(s) and other storage devices are displayed.
3	Close Windows Explorer	
4	Click **Start** and choose your user account name	This time, Windows Explorer opens to your personal folders. Among these folders are My Documents, My Music, My Pictures, and My Videos.
5	Double-click **My Documents**	To open the folder.
6	Open **Student Data**	This folder contains several unit folders.
7	Open the current unit folder	The folder contains several files and subfolders.
	Observe the Address bar	It shows the path to the current unit folder.
8	In the Address bar, click as shown	Student Data ▾ Unit_03 ▸ / Unit_01 / Unit_02 / hare with ▾ You can click one of these triangles to see a folder's contents. The current folder is highlighted in the list.
9	In the Address bar, click **Student Data**	You can use the Address bar to navigate to different folders in a path.
10	Open the current unit folder again	
	Click **Garden Gate**	To select it.
11	On the Command bar, click [button]	(The "Show preview pane" button.) To display the preview pane. It provides a quick way to view your files without having to open them in an application they're associated with.
	Click **Report**	(In the contents pane.) To preview the document. The preview pane makes locating specific content fast and convenient.
	Close the preview pane	On the Command bar, click the "Show preview pane" button again.

12 Observe the details pane	(At the bottom of the window.) The details pane shows various information about a selected file, including the file type, the size, and the date it was last modified.
13 Close Windows Explorer	

Libraries

Explanation

In Windows 7, every computer has four Public folders that all users of a PC can access. These folders are named Public Documents, Public Music, Public Pictures, and Public Videos. Every user account has its own personal folders, which are accessible only to the individual user and the computer administrator.

Every user account also has four default libraries, organized by content type. They are labeled Documents, Music, Pictures, and Videos, as shown in Exhibit 3-2. A Windows *library* is a named collection of folders grouped for organizational purposes. Libraries aggregate related files from various locations, including shared files on your network, and display them in a central location. For example, if you have two Microsoft Word documents in your My Documents folder and there are three Notepad documents in the Public Documents folder, you'll see all five documents in the Documents library.

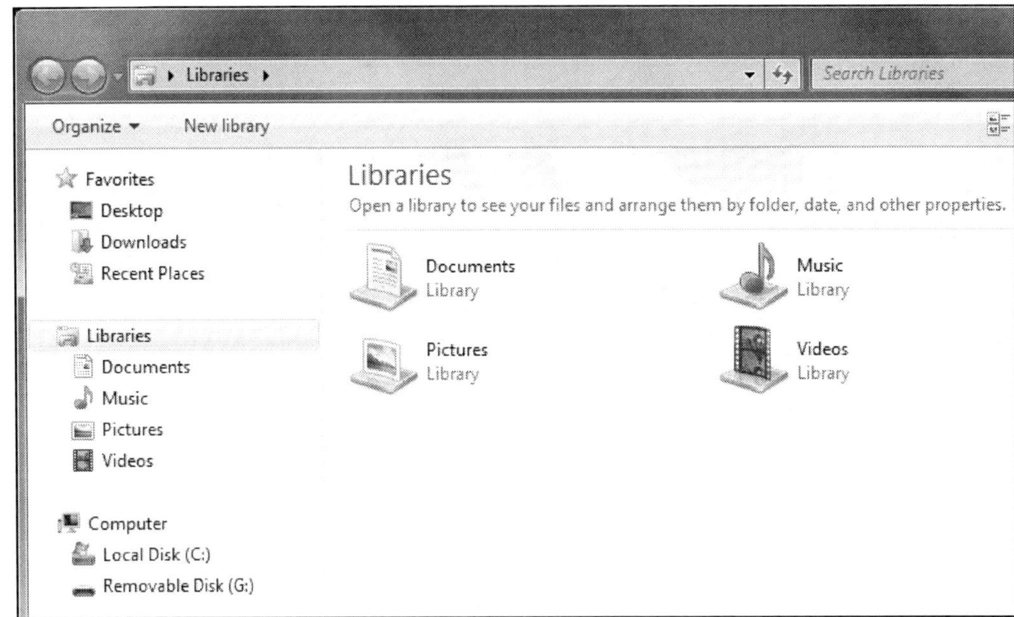

Exhibit 3-2: There are four default libraries for organizing files by general type

In previous versions of Windows, you could have documents in multiple folders and subfolders with no way to view or access all files of a particular type. In Windows 7, it doesn't matter where a particular file is physically stored—you can access it in its corresponding library. The Documents library, for example, shows all text-related files, including documents, PDFs, and spreadsheets, stored in the default locations and any additional locations you specify.

Viewing a library's locations

To see which folders are included in a library, select the library in the navigation pane in Windows Explorer. The number of included locations appears as a "# locations" link under the library's title in the contents pane. Click the link to open the Library Locations dialog box for that library and see the full path to each location where the files are physically stored, as shown in Exhibit 3-3.

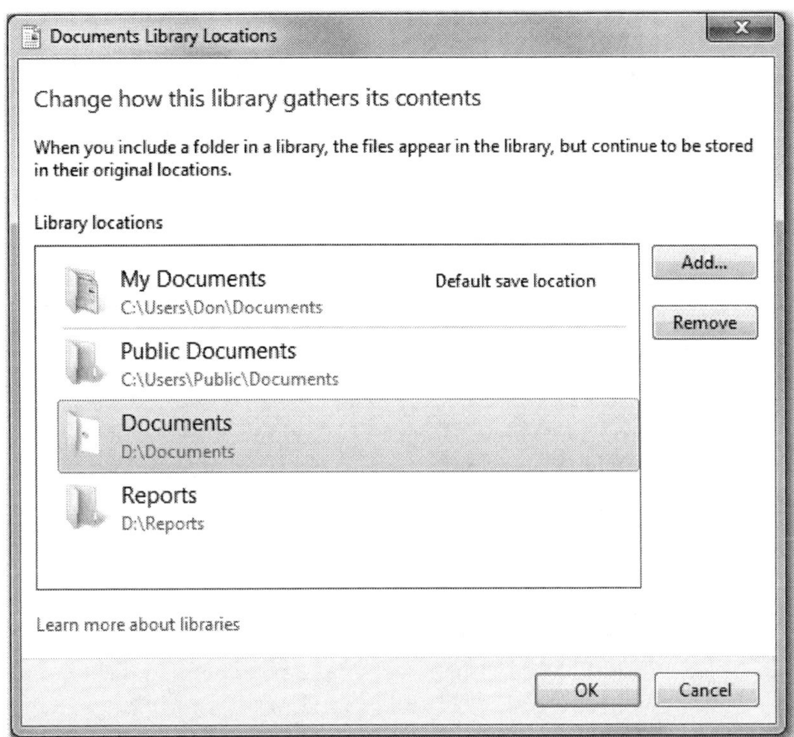

Exhibit 3-3: You can see all of the locations that make up a library

Creating and deleting libraries

You can create your own libraries to set up convenient collections of files from multiple storage locations, and you can add your own folders to a library. For example, if you like to store all your documents in a folder on an external hard drive, you can add that folder to your Documents library.

To create a library, do either of the following:

- In the navigation pane of Windows Explorer, select Libraries. On the Command bar, click New library and enter a name. You can then add locations to your new library.
- Right-click a folder and choose "Include in library," "Create new library." This action automatically creates a library with the name of the selected folder and includes it. You can then add more locations as needed.

To delete a library, select it in Windows Explorer and press Delete, or right-click it and choose Delete. Deleting a library does not remove any of the files or folders that were included in it.

Adding folders to a library

To add a location to a library, follow these steps:

1. In the navigation pane of Windows Explorer, select the library to which you want to add a location.
2. In the contents pane, under the library's title, click the "# locations" link to open the Library Locations dialog box, shown in Exhibit 3-3.
3. Click Add. Navigate to and select the desired folder, and click the Include folder button. You are returned to the Library Locations dialog box with the new folder shown.
4. Click OK.

You can also right-click a folder in Windows Explorer and choose "Include in library," and then select the library you want. You can add a folder to more than one library.

Removing folders from a library

To remove a folder from a library:

- Right-click the folder and choose "Remove location from library."
- With the library displayed in the contents pane, click the "# locations" link under the library's title. Then use the Library Locations dialog box to remove the folder.

Default save locations and display order

Every library has a default save location—the actual folder that stores files saved in a library. For example, if you drag a text file to the Documents library, the file will be saved in the My Documents folder by default. You can change the default save location in the Library Locations dialog box. Right-click a folder and choose "Set as default save location."

You can also use the Library Locations dialog box to change the order in which locations appear in the contents pane. By default, these folders appear in the order in which they were added to the library. To change the order, right-click a folder in the Library Locations dialog box and choose Move up or Move down.

Do it!

A-2: Using libraries

Here's how	Here's why
1 On the taskbar, click the Windows Explorer icon	Windows Explorer opens to the four default libraries by default.
2 In the navigation pane, under Libraries, click **Documents**	To select the Documents library. The Student Data folder appears in the contents pane. This folder is stored in the My Documents folder.
3 Click as shown	Pictures My Pictures Public Pictures To expand the Pictures library. It includes My Pictures and Public Pictures.
4 In the navigation pane, click **My Pictures**	The folder is empty.
Click **Public Pictures**	A Sample Pictures folder is displayed in the contents pane. This is a folder of stock images that comes installed with Windows 7.
5 Open **Sample Pictures**	To see the pictures in the folder.
6 In the navigation pane, click **Pictures**	To return to the Pictures library.
7 Under the Pictures library title, click **2 locations**	To open the Pictures Library Locations dialog box. My Pictures is the default save location. If you save or move something to the Pictures library, it's stored in the My Pictures folder by default.
Click **Add**	You'll add another location to this library.
8 Navigate to the current unit folder	Open My Documents, Student Data, and then the current unit folder. It contains the folders Reports and Spice Pics.
9 Select **Spice Pics** and click **Include folder**	(The Include folder button is at the bottom of the dialog box.) You are returned to the Pictures Library Locations dialog box, and Spice Pics is now included.
10 In the dialog box, right-click **Spice Pics** and choose **Move up**	To move it up in the Pictures library.

11 Click **OK**	To close the dialog box and return to Windows Explorer.
Observe the contents pane	The Pictures library now includes the images in the Spice Pics folder.
Observe the navigation pane	The Spice Pics folder is displayed under the Pictures library.
12 In the navigation pane, click **Libraries**	You'll create a library.
On the Command bar, click **New library**	
Type **Work Reports** and press ENTER	 Work Reports Library Work Reports is displayed as a library.
13 Double-click **Work Reports**	The window indicates that the library is empty (no locations have been specified for it).
Click **Include a folder**	
Navigate to the current unit folder	
14 Select **Reports**	
Click **Include folder**	 Work Reports library Includes: 1 location Name Reports (2) C:\Users\Computer01\My Documents\Student Earnings Sales The Work Reports library is displayed.
Observe the navigation pane	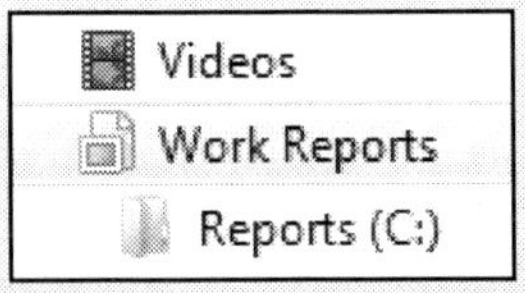 Videos Work Reports Reports (C:)
15 Under the Work Reports library title, click **1 location**	This library currently shows files from only one location.

	Here's how	Here's why
	16 Click **Add**	
	In the navigation pane, expand Documents	
	Select **My Documents**	
	Click **Include folder**	
	17 Right-click **My Documents** and choose **Set as default save location**	
	Click **OK**	My Documents is now included in the Work Reports library. A folder can be included in more than one library.
	18 In the navigation pane, select **Work Reports**	(If necessary.) You'll delete this library.
	Press DELETE	A message box asks if you're sure you want to delete the folder.
	Click **Yes**	The Libraries folder displays the four default libraries.
Ask the class this question. It's important to the understanding of libraries.	19 Were the files in the Work Reports library also deleted?	***No, they are still in the folders where they are actually stored.***
	20 Close Windows Explorer	

Topic B: Working with Windows Explorer

Explanation

There are many ways to customize the way you see files, folders, and other information in Windows Explorer. You can customize view settings and change file and folder properties.

Windows Explorer settings

You can change the way Windows Explorer displays objects. For example, you can display files as icons or thumbnails; you can display file details; or you can display a simple list of files. You can sort, group, and filter files, and you can show or hide various panes in Windows Explorer.

Changing view options

To change the way items are shown in the contents pane, either click the View button to switch to the next view option, or click the down-arrow next to the View button and use the slider, shown in Exhibit 3-4.

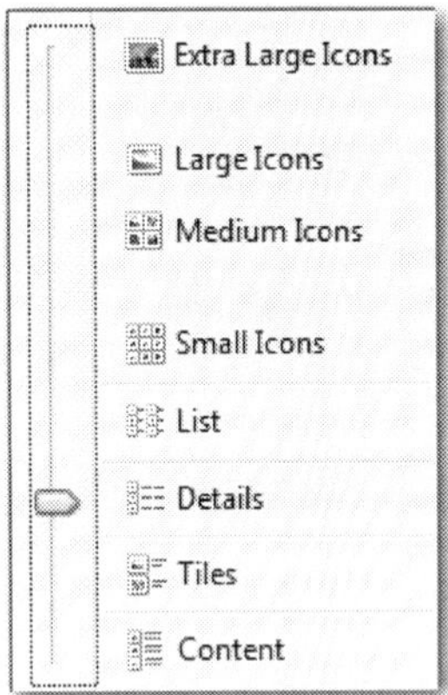

Exhibit 3-4: View options

Changing the layout

To show or hide various panes in Windows Explorer, click Organize and choose Layout; then choose the panes you want to show or hide. You cannot hide the contents pane.

Sorting and arranging files

With Windows 7, you can sort, group, and filter files based on file properties, including name, creation date, size, and author. These options enable you to easily work with large sets of files and find the files you need.

Customizing column headings

The Windows Explorer contents pane has columns that list various file properties, such as the file's name, type, and size. The columns that are available by default depend on the folder type (e.g., music, documents, pictures). For example, a music folder or library shows the file name, artists, album name, number, and song title by default. You can add and remove columns as needed.

To add or remove columns, right-click any column heading. The shortcut menu shows common headings for that folder type, and you can check or clear headings as needed. You can also choose More to open the Choose Details dialog box, shown in Exhibit 3-5. This dialog box provides a complete list of available headings.

You can also resize and rearrange columns:

- To resize just two columns, point to the border between the two column headings; when the pointer changes to a double-headed arrow, drag left or right.
- To make columns just wide enough to display their data, right-click a column heading and choose either "Size column to fit" or "Size all columns to fit."
- To change the order of the columns, drag column headings left or right.

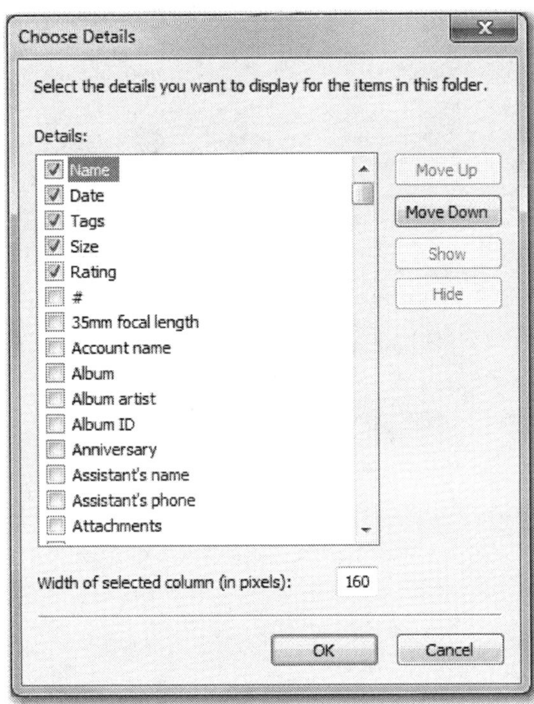

Exhibit 3-5: You can choose which column headings appear in the contents pane

Sorting and filtering files

You can sort files and folders by any details shown, in either ascending or descending order, by clicking the column heading. To switch between ascending and descending order, click the column heading.

You can also filter the items shown in a window. For example, you can display only those files with names starting with A-H. To filter your view of files and folders, click the arrow to the right of a column heading and check the desired filter options.

Arranging files

In Windows 7, you can arrange, or "stack," files with similar attributes. For example, you could create stacks from a selection of music files according to the music genre. Rather than seeing a large list of files or icons, you would see stacks of related files. In Exhibit 3-6, image files are stacked by the month they were created in.

Stacks act like folders—if you double-click a stack, you'll see all the files in it. To arrange items into stacks, click the down-arrow next to the "Arrange by" label in the contents pane, and select an option.

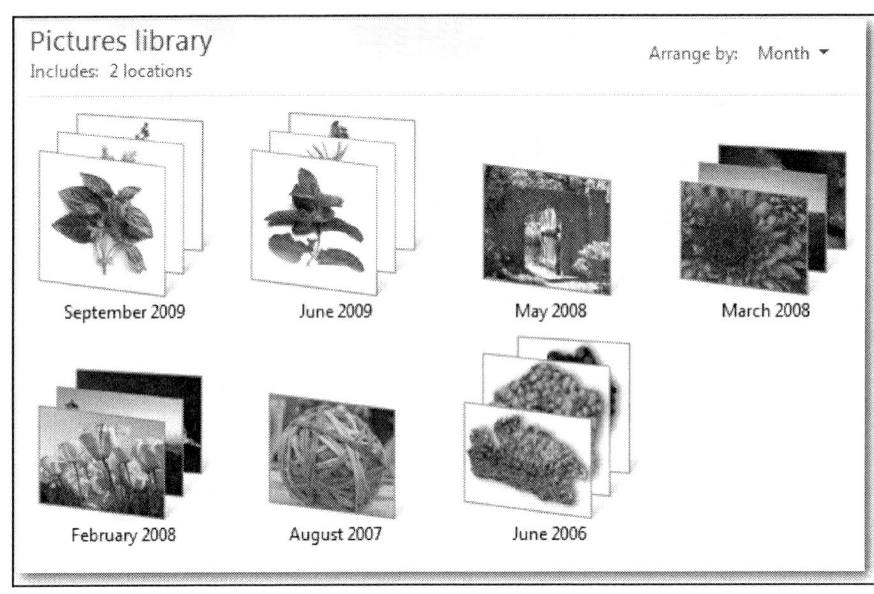

Exhibit 3-6: Image files stacked by the month they were created in

Do it!

B-1: Customizing Windows Explorer

Here's how	Here's why
1 Click **Start** and choose **Pictures**	To open the Pictures library.
2 Click the arrow next to the View button, as shown	To open the slider.
Drag the slider to **Details**	In the contents pane, more file details are displayed.
3 Observe the column headings	Default columns for picture folders are Name, Date, Tags, Size, and Rating.
4 Click the **Size** column heading	Files are now sorted from largest to smallest. A small arrow above the heading points down, indicating descending order.
Click **Size** again	The order is reversed to ascending order—the arrow above the heading now points up.
5 Click the **Name** heading	The files are in alphabetical order (folders are displayed first).
6 Click the arrow to the right of the Name column, as shown	Name / Date / Basil / Cinnamon / Cloves / A – H / I – P / Q – Z
Check **A-H**	Only files whose names begin with A-H are displayed.
Check **Q-Z**	Both subsets are displayed.
Clear both checkboxes	To see all the files again.
7 Press ESC	To close the checkboxes. (You can also click away from the list.)
8 Right-click any column heading	A shortcut menu opens. The checked items are the current detail columns.
Clear **Tags**	To hide the Tags column.
9 Right-click a column heading	
Clear **Rating**	To hide the Ratings column.

10	Right-click a column heading and choose **More...**	To open the Choose Details dialog box.
	Scroll down and check **Dimensions**	To display the Dimensions column.
	Click **OK**	The Dimensions column is displayed; it shows the picture size in pixels.
11	Select the **Music** library and open the Sample Music folder	Windows 7 includes a few sample music files.
	Observe the column headings	The default headings for music folders are Name, Contributing artists, Album, #, and Title. The changes you made in the Pictures library do not apply to other windows.
12	From the Arrange by list, select **Genre**	The songs are arranged into virtual folders, or stacks, by genre.

File details and metadata

Explanation

Some of what you see in the detail columns are general file properties, like file size, file type, and creation date. These properties are descriptions of the file and usually aren't manually changed. File size, for example, is a description of how much space the file takes up on the hard disk. You wouldn't change this manually; it changes when the file is edited and becomes bigger or smaller.

Metadata

Files often have *metadata*—data about the data—stored in the file. Metadata provides extra information about a file or folder. For example, when you take a picture with your digital camera, various details about the photo are saved within the picture file, as shown in Exhibit 3-7. A digital camera typically records the date, time, exposure settings, and other details that make up an image file's metadata. Song files contain the artist, songwriter, publisher, album art, and digital rights management information.

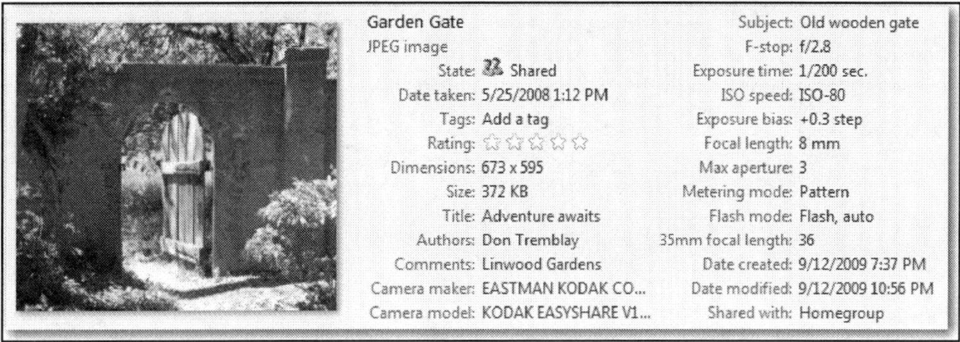

Exhibit 3-7: Metadata for a picture, with the details pane expanded

Windows 7 enables you to record metadata for any file on your computer. General file properties are recorded automatically, such as the date the file was created, its size, and so forth. Details that you can add include the author, rating, and genre. Some details—for example, a camera's f-stop or focal length—cannot be changed, and you wouldn't need to. You can protect a file's metadata from unintended changes by making the file read-only.

To add or edit standard metadata for a file:

1. Select a file or folder in the contents pane.
2. If necessary, display the details pane and drag it upward to make it larger. The wider you expand the folder window, the more standard metadata details will be displayed.
3. In the details pane, click the desired metadata field and enter the new value.

You can also view file properties and change metadata by right-clicking a file and choosing Properties, and then activating the Details tab of the Properties dialog box.

Do it!

B-2: Editing metadata

Here's how	Here's why
1 Navigate to the current unit folder	
Click **Garden Gate**	To select it. The file has a lot of metadata that is not displayed.
2 Right-click the details pane	To open a shortcut menu.
Choose **Size**, **Large**	
Maximize the window	(If necessary.) More metadata is displayed in the details pane.
3 Click **Rubberband Ball**	This file has metadata, but most fields are empty.
4 In the details pane, click **Add a title**	You'll edit this detail.
Enter a title of your choice	
Press ENTER	(Or click Save.) To save the information.
5 Click to the right of Comments	
Type a comment and press ENTER	
6 Close the window	

If the Comments field is not visible, tell students to drag the top of the details pane upward to enlarge it.

Topic C: Searching for content

Explanation

Windows 7 makes searching for content on your computer fast and easy. You can search for content by using the Start menu and Windows Explorer. The search box in the Start menu will find installed programs and files in indexed folders and libraries. Windows Explorer will search the selected folder or storage device, even if it's not indexed.

Indexing

Windows creates and maintains an index of file names, contents, and metadata for faster searching. When you search with keywords, Windows searches the index rather than the actual files, making the search faster in most cases.

By default, Windows indexes folders included in libraries and other frequently used folders. Program and system folders are not usually indexed. These are typically large and rarely searched folders; indexing them will usually slow down searches.

Managing indexed locations

The simplest way to ensure that a folder is indexed for search results is to include it in a library, because all library folders are indexed automatically. When you search a folder that's not indexed, Windows offers you the option of adding it to the index. But be careful not to do this for folders you don't search regularly—it might slow down your future searches.

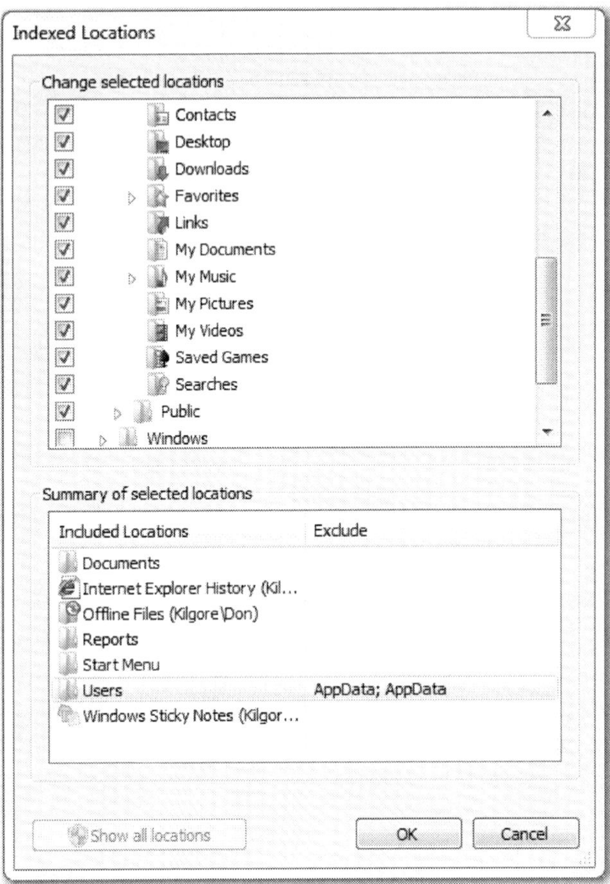

Exhibit 3-8: The Indexed Locations dialog box

To see or change which folders are indexed:

1 Click Start, type "index" in the search box, and click Indexing Options to open the Indexing Options dialog box.
2 Click Modify to open the Indexed Locations dialog box, shown in Exhibit 3-8. Here, you can add or remove locations.

You might not need to use this dialog box often, but if you ever add a large folder or system folder to the index, you'll probably want to remove it from the index later so that it doesn't slow down your everyday search operations.

Folder search options

Other important search settings are found on the Search tab of the Folder Options dialog box, shown in Exhibit 3-9. These settings determine how Windows searches folders:

- **What to search** — By default, Windows searches for file names only. If you want to find words or phrases within documents that are in non-indexed locations, you'll need to change this setting.
- **How to search** — Specify whether to search subfolders and to return partial matches.
- **When searching non-indexed locations** — Specify whether to include system folders and compressed files when searching non-indexed locations.

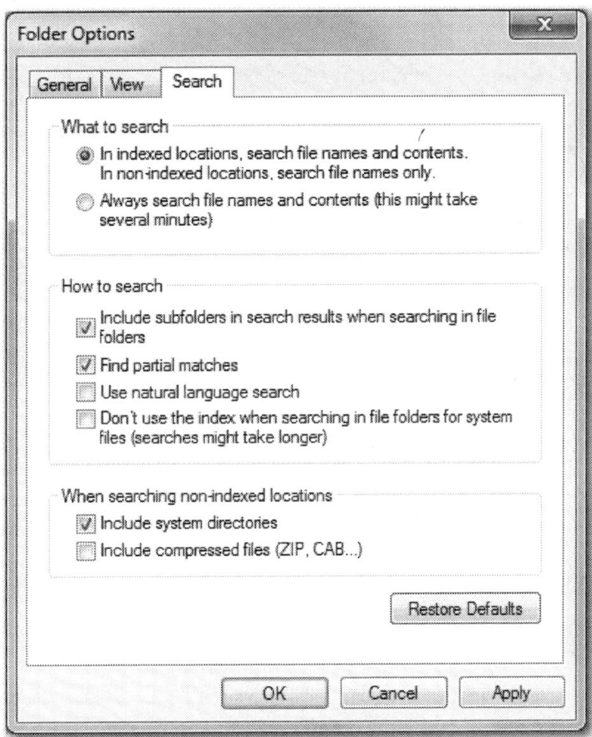

Exhibit 3-9: The Search tab in the Folder Options dialog box

Searching from the Start menu

When you open the Start menu, the insertion point is automatically placed in the Search box so you can type search criteria immediately. You can search for files and programs. In a way, the Search box replaces the Run command from earlier versions of Windows. For example, if you click Start, type "calc," and press Enter, the Calculator program opens.

If you're looking for a system file or a document on an external flash drive, you'll need to search in Windows Explorer.

Searching in Windows Explorer

In the upper right-corner of Windows Explorer is a search box that will search whatever folder or device is selected in the navigation pane and shown in the contents pane. This search method looks through file names, file properties and metadata, and file contents, when applicable.

These details can be searched whether or not the folders are indexed. If they are not indexed, the search might take longer, and a prompt at the top of the contents pane will ask if you want to add the folder to the index.

Search techniques

Here are a few tips to refine your searches:

- **Use wildcards** — Wildcards are symbols that take the place of other letters. An asterisk (*) represents zero or more letters. By default, the search will return partial matches, but only at the beginning of a word, not in the middle or at the end. For instance, searching on **proj** will return "Project" and "projected"; searching on ***ject** will return these, as well as "reject" and "rejected"; searching on **ject** will not return any of these.
- **Use quotation marks** — Sometimes you can find a document by remembering a phrase in it. If you start your search terms with a quotation mark ("), only examples of those words in that order will be returned. So, entering **high school** will return any documents with both words, whether or not they are together, while searching on **"high school** will return only results with that exact phrase.
- **Filter the search** — You can refine a search by specifying things like date modified, file size, and file type. The filters available change depending on which files are in the unfiltered results.

Searches are not case sensitive, even if quotation marks are used.

Saving your searches

If you often perform the same search in the same location, you can save that search for future reference. Recent search terms are saved in the search box, but saving a search retains both the terms and the location.

To save a search you have completed, click Save search on the Command bar and enter a name. Saved searches are listed under Favorites in the navigation pane.

Do it!

C-1: Searching for file names and contents

Here's how	Here's why
1 Click **Start**	
Type **status**	The search finds several programs in the Control Panel, as well as a document named Status.
2 From the taskbar, open Windows Explorer	It opens to the libraries.
Click **Search Libraries**	To place the insertion point.
3 Type **status**	Windows Explorer highlights every instance of the word "status" found in the libraries, but does not return programs like the Start menu does.
4 Click in the search box and type **proj**	Windows Explorer highlights all instances of the partial word "proj" within the contents of library files. Two documents contain the word "project."
Double-click **Report**	To open the file directly from the search results.
Close WordPad	
5 On the Command bar, click **Save Search**	The default name is "proj."
Type **project**	To rename the search to be more specific.
Click **Save**	Favorites Desktop Downloads Recent Places project The saved search appears under Favorites. You can run this search any time by clicking it.
6 Click in the search box and type **annual report**	Two documents are found that contain both words.
Click the search box	To select the text
7 Type **"annual rep**	This time, only one document is found that contains both words in that order. The other document contained both "annual" and "report" but not the phrase "annual report."
8 Close Windows Explorer	

Point out that renaming a search is optional, but sometimes students might want to indicate the complete search term.

Be sure students enter the starting quotation mark.

Unit summary: Folders, libraries, and content

Topic A In this topic, you learned about the new design features of **Windows Explorer**, and you learned about **libraries**. You learned that libraries are collections of related files and folders from various physical locations. You learned how to create and delete libraries, view a library's storage locations, add a folder to a library, remove a folder from a library, and change the default save location for a library.

Topic B In this topic, you learned how to **customize Windows Explorer** to arrange and display files and folders as needed. You also learned how to display and edit file **metadata**.

Topic C In this topic, you learned how to **search** for files and content on your computer. You learned that Windows **indexes** some folders to make searching fast, and you learned about the differences between searching from the Start menu and searching in Windows Explorer. Finally, you learned how to save searches.

Review questions

1 If a library has more than one folder, how can you tell which folder is the default save location?

Open the Library Locations dialog box.

2 A different user account on your computer has two documents in the My Documents folder, and five documents in the Public Documents folder. You have no documents of your own yet. How many documents will be displayed if you open the Documents library from your user account?

The five documents the other user placed in the Public Documents folder. You would not have access to files in another user account without administrator privileges.

3 True or false? A folder can be included in only one library at a time.

False.

4 If you right-click a folder and choose "Include in library," "Create new library," what will the default name of the new library be?

A New Library

B Library01

C It depends on folder contents

D The same as the folder name

5 Clicking a column heading does what?

A Sorts the files on that column

B Expands and collapses the column

C Opens the Column Heading dialog box

D Makes a clicking sound

6 True or false? Different folder types show different detail columns.

True. Different folder types might display different details, but the columns can be changed.

7 True or false? The details shown in the details pane are stored in Windows Explorer. The data is not copied when you copy the file to another system.

False. Metadata is stored within the file itself.

8 True or false? If you add a folder to the Documents library, it will be indexed automatically.

True. Folders in libraries are indexed automatically.

9 True or false? If you want to search the internal contents of files in a folder, you need to index the folder first.

False. This is the default setting, but you can set Windows so it searches contents in non-indexed locations, too.

10 Entering **oin** in the search box would return which of the following? [Choose all that apply.]

A coin

B oink

C tenderloin

D appointment

E ointment

11 If you want to search for a specific phrase, you should enter search terms starting with what symbol?

A *

B =

C >

D “

Independent practice activity

In this activity, you'll practice navigating the computer contents, change the way Windows Explorer displays files and information about files, and perform a simple search from the Start menu.

1 Open Windows Explorer. In the navigation pane, select Computer. What is the total capacity and free space of the C: drive? What other drives and devices do you see?

Answers will vary, but students will probably see at least a DVD drive.

2 Select the Pictures library, and change the view to Large Icons.

3 Change the view back to Details, and remove the Dimensions column. Add the Type column. Set all columns to fit their data.

4 Rearrange the columns as follows: Name, Type, Size, Date.

5 From the Arrange by list, select Month.

6 In the current unit folder, select the picture Rubberband Ball. Expand the details pane, if necessary.

7 In the metadata, enter your name as the author and click Save.

8 Close all open windows.

9 Click Start. Type your name in the search box. Click the picture name in the menu.

10 Close the picture.

Unit 4

Device Stage

Unit time: 30 minutes

Complete this unit, and you'll know how to:

A Work with your devices and install a local printer.

Topic A: Devices and printers

Explanation

Windows 7 makes it easy to interact with your devices and gadgets, including cell phones, digital cameras, USB flash drives, printers, and music players, all from a central location—the Devices and Printers window. In addition, device manufacturers can provide detailed information for their devices so that clicking a device icon opens a device-specific window with images, information, and resources that the device manufacturer can control and update. This new feature is called *Device Stage*.

Interacting with your devices

To interact with an external device, simply plug it into the appropriate port on your computer. When you connect a device for the first time, Windows automatically loads the required drivers, so you can interact with the device immediately. (*Drivers* are small software programs that enable a device to communicate with the operating system.) If Windows does not have the driver for a particular device, it searches online for it; if Windows finds the driver, it installs it automatically. In addition to direct connections via cables, devices can also connect automatically via a wireless network or Bluetooth.

Device Stage

Once a supported device is connected and its drivers installed, a photo-realistic icon appears on the taskbar, and a window specific to that device opens. Point to the taskbar icon to display its thumbnail, as shown in Exhibit 4-1, or click it to minimize the Device Stage window. You can also right-click the icon to open the Jump List, which contains several device-specific commands and options.

Exhibit 4-1: When you connect a supported device, an icon appears on the taskbar

The heightened device awareness and feature set of Windows 7 is called *Device Stage*, and it has three components:

- **A taskbar icon** — Exhibit 4-1 shows the taskbar icon and thumbnail of a Device Stage–supported device—in this case, a Brother printer.

  Not all Device Stage–supported devices will appear on the taskbar; some devices that are always connected, such as a mouse, don't call for a taskbar icon.
- **An icon in the Devices and Printers window** — Like all other installed devices, icons for your Device Stage–supported devices appear in this window. Some device icons will appear in this window only when the device is connected.
- **An XML-based page of links, images, and frequently used commands** — When you connect a supported device, Windows quickly recognizes it, installs the required drivers, and opens this specialized page. (Again, this is for Device Stage–supported devices only.)

Exhibit 4-2 shows a printer's Device Stage window, providing easy access to frequently used commands. In the Device Stage window for a music player, for example, there would be links to browse files, import images, and synchronize music between the device and your PC.

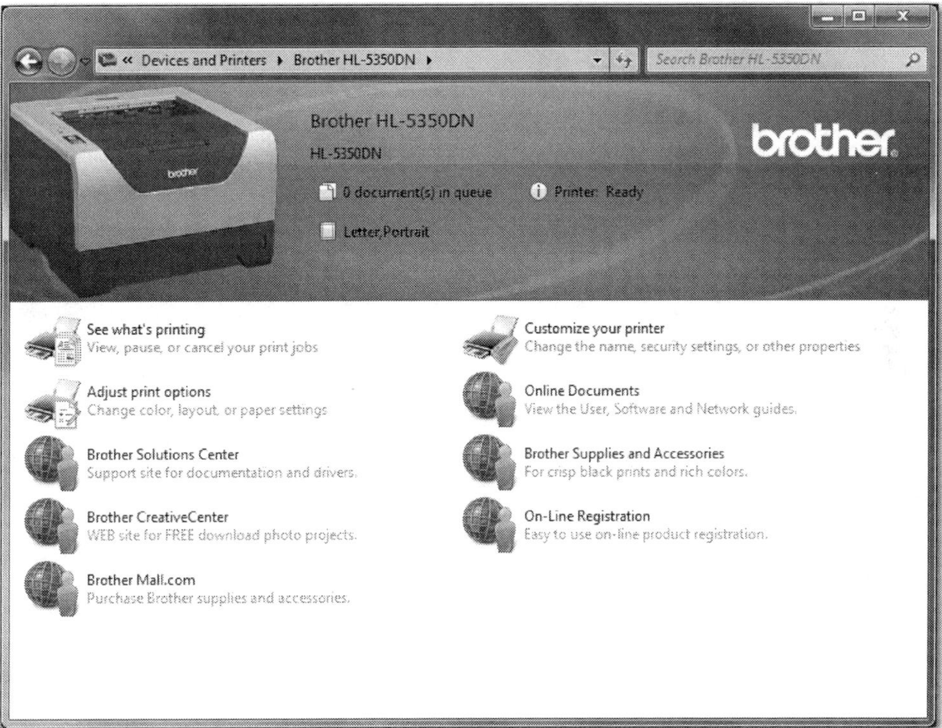

Exhibit 4-2: The Device Stage window for the Brother HL 5350DN printer

Windows stores the images and information for many popular devices, and regularly updates its database of devices behind the scenes. As mentioned earlier, this content is provided by device manufacturers. If a device manufacturer creates or updates Device Stage content, Windows downloads it automatically if your computer is connected to the Internet.

The Devices and Printers window

The Devices and Printers window provides a central location where you can view and access all of your computer's devices. You'll see photo-realistic icons representing your Device Stage–supported devices, and generic icons for other devices. There's also an icon for the computer itself—a laptop computer displays a laptop icon, as shown in Exhibit 4-3, and a desktop computer will display either a hard-drive icon or a desktop-PC icon. To open the Devices and Printers window, click Start and choose Devices and Printers.

Exhibit 4-3: The Devices and Printers window

You can perform a variety of tasks in the Devices and Printers window, depending on the device. For example, you can open files stored on a USB drive, view documents waiting to print, or synchronize files on a music player. You can view detailed information about a device, determine whether a device is working properly, and connect network devices and printers that were not added automatically.

You can click a device icon to display device-specific options on the command bar. You can also configure how Windows interacts with a device. For example, you can set a digital camera to automatically import all pictures and videos whenever you connect it to the computer.

The Devices and Printers window does not include internal components such as sound cards, video cards, or hard disks. To view or manage those devices, use Device Manager in the Control Panel.

Devices not supported by Device Stage

At the time of this writing, a limited number of devices had Device Stage content prepared for Windows 7 users. Support will continue to expand over time.

If a device is not yet Device Stage–enabled, the AutoPlay dialog box will open when you connect the device to your computer. AutoPlay provides general options for interacting with devices. You can click an option or close the AutoPlay dialog box. In the Devices and Printers window, double-clicking a device not supported by Device Stage will open the Properties dialog box for that device.

If a device is not working properly, its icon will display a yellow triangle with an exclamation point. Right-click the icon and choose Troubleshoot; Windows will attempt to resolve the problem.

Do it!

A-1: Exploring devices

Here's how	Here's why
1 Log on to your user account	If necessary.
2 Click **Start** and choose **Devices and Printers**	To open the Devices and Printers window. Icons for your computer's devices are displayed. Windows includes default icons for a fax and a printer.
3 Click the icon for your computer	(Click the icon for Computer##.) A device summary is displayed at the bottom of the window.
4 Double-click the icon for your computer	The Properties dialog box opens.
Activate the Hardware tab	The Hardware tab displays a complete list of your computer's internal components.
Click **Cancel**	To close the Properties dialog box.
5 Right-click the computer icon	To display a list of commands and options.
Choose **Device installation settings**	
Read the dialog box	By default, Windows automatically downloads updated drivers and icons for your devices. If a manufacturer has made Device Stage content available, Windows will download the files automatically.
6 Click **Cancel**	To close the dialog box without making any changes.

If the computers are Device Stage–enabled, a content page will open instead of the Properties dialog box.

Tell students to leave the Devices and Printers window open, and point out that there are no Device Stage–supported devices currently connected to the PC.

Installing and troubleshooting devices

Explanation

As we mentioned earlier, when you connect a device for the first time, Windows automatically loads the required drivers and related device information, allowing you to interact with the device immediately. However, if Windows does not recognize a device or does not install drivers automatically, there are a few simple steps you can take to resolve the problem and start using your device:

- Make sure that your system is connected to the Internet.
- Check to see whether optional updates are available. To do so, open the Control Panel, click System and Security, and click Windows Update. If there's a link indicating that optional updates are available, click it, and check the update list to see if an update for your device is available.
- Verify that automatic updating is fully enabled. In the left pane of the Windows Update window, click Change settings. Verify that "Recommended updates" is checked; if it's not, check it.
- Download a driver directly from the device manufacturer's Web site. Double-click the installation file and follow the prompts to install the driver.

Do it!

A-2: Installing a device

Before class, test the devices students will use to ensure that the activity works as planned. Try to use devices that support Device Stage. If multiple devices are not available, conduct a demonstration, using a Device Stage–supported device.

Depending on the device, you might need to have students skip to step 6.

Ask students if anyone sees a yellow triangle on one of their device icons. If so, have the student right-click the icon and choose Troubleshoot to try to resolve the problem.

Here's how

1 Obtain a device from your instructor. Follow your instructor's directions to connect it to the computer.

2 In the notification area, read the pop-up window to observe how Windows finds and installs the required driver.

3 Is the device supported by Device Stage? How can you tell?

If a device icon appears on the taskbar and a window specific to that device opens, the device is supported by Device Stage.

4 If the device is supported by Device Stage and an icon appears on the taskbar, follow your instructor's lead and explore the device options.

5 If the device is supported by Device Stage, click one or more links to information and resources about the device.

6 If the AutoPlay dialog box opens after you connect the device, follow your instructor's lead to explore the device or close the dialog box.

7 Locate the device icon in the Devices and Printers window.

8 Click each device icon and observe how the Command bar changes for each device.

9 Do any of the device icons shown in the Devices and Printers window display a yellow triangle?

Devices that are not working properly will display such an icon. You can right-click the device icon and choose Troubleshoot, and Windows will attempt to fix the problem.

Installing a local printer

Explanation

In Windows, the term *printer* includes the set of software components that manage the printing process. To Windows, your actual printer (the output equipment) is considered a *print device*. Windows makes it easy to connect to local and network printers and manage your print output.

Installing a printer in Windows 7 is simple. In many cases, all you need to do is plug the cable of your print device into your computer. Windows recognizes the print device and installs the latest drivers automatically.

If you have a printing device that Windows does not recognize, or if you want to add a network printer, you can do so by using the Add Printer Wizard, which walks you through a short series of steps.

The Add Printer Wizard

To add a printer with the Add Printer Wizard:

1 Click Start and choose Devices and Printers.
2 At the top of the window, click "Add a printer." (You can also right-click an empty area of the Devices and Printers window and choose "Add a printer.")
3 Follow the wizard's instructions to install the printer. When the process is completed, a printer icon resembling the output device will appear in the Devices and Printers window.

You can add a printer through the Add Printer Wizard without actually having the printing device connected.

The default printer

When you install your first printer, it becomes the default printer, indicated by a green checkmark, as shown in Exhibit 4-4. The *default printer* is the printer that programs print to by default. If only one printer is installed, it's automatically the default printer. Only one printer can be the default, and all print jobs are sent to the default printer unless otherwise specified.

Keep in mind that some programs have commands that send print jobs directly to the default printer without giving you a chance to choose an alternate printer, so it's important that you have the right printer assigned as the default.

Exhibit 4-4: The default printer is indicated by a green checkmark

Changing the default printer

If you have multiple printers and you need to switch between them, you can easily change the default printer. Right-click the icon for the printer that you want to set as the default, and choose "Set as default printer." Otherwise, when you want to print a document from a program, you can directly specify the alternate printer in the program's Print dialog box.

Do it!

A-3: Installing a local printer

The Devices and Printers window is open.

TIPS Students can also right-click a blank area of the window and choose "Add a printer."

You can also have students install a USB printer that Windows will recognize and install automatically.

It's important that students select this printer because it's supported by Device Stage.

TIPS You can change the default printer by right-clicking the printer icon and choosing "Set as default printer."

Here's how	Here's why
1 Observe the default printer	The green checkmark indicates the default printer. The Microsoft XPS Document Writer and a fax are already installed as part of Window 7.
On the Command bar, click **Add a printer**	To start the Add Printer Wizard.
2 Click **Add a local printer**	
3 Verify that **LPT1: (Printer Port)** is selected	In the "Use an existing port" list.
Click **Next**	After a moment, a list of manufacturers and printers is displayed. Windows 7 has a large library of printer drivers to make the installation process easy.
4 From the Manufacturer list, select **Brother**	
From the Printers list, select **Brother HL-5380DN**	Scroll down the list.
Click **Next**	
5 In the Printer name box, type **My printer**	To name the printer.
Click **Next**	
Verify that **Set as the default printer** is selected	If available. If this is the first printer installed on the computer, it's set as the default automatically.
6 Click **Finish**	My printer The new printer is added, and the checkmark indicates that it's the default printer.
7 Open the printer	(Double-click the icon.) This printer model supports Device Stage, so it opens in a specialized window with content provided by its manufacturer.

8 Observe the taskbar	Device Stage–supported printers and devices have a taskbar icon when open.
Click the taskbar icon	To minimize the Device Stage window.
Right-click the printer icon	To open the printer's Jump List. From here, you can access a variety of device-specific commands and options.
Click **Close window**	To close the window from the Jump List.

Unit summary: Device Stage

Topic A

In this topic, you learned how to interact with and manage devices, and you learned about **Device Stage**. You learned how to install devices and install a local printer.

Review questions

1 True or false? For most devices, when you connect a device for the first time, Windows automatically loads the required drivers.

True

2 True or false? Device manufacturers provide the XML content for Device Stage.

True. When a device manufacturer creates or updates Device Stage content, Windows downloads it automatically if your computer is connected to the Internet.

3 Which window provides a central location you can use to view and access all of your computer's devices?

Devices and Printers

4 True or false? If a device is not yet Device Stage–enabled, the AutoPlay dialog box opens when you connect the device to your computer.

True. The AutoPlay dialog box provides general options for interacting with the device.

5 True or false? If a device is not yet Device Stage–enabled, double-clicking its icon in the Devices and Printers window opens the Properties dialog box for that device.

True

Independent practice activity

In this activity, you will manage devices and printers.

1 Obtain a USB device and connect it to your computer. Windows will most likely recognize the device and install the required drivers automatically. If Windows does not recognize it and install drivers after a minute or so, obtain the drivers manually.

2 If the device is supported by Device Stage, customize how Windows interacts with the device when you connect it.

3 Add the printer **Canon Inkjet MP980**.

4 Is the printer supported by Device Stage? How can you tell?

Yes. When you double-click the printer icon, a specialized window opens, and an icon appears on the taskbar.

5 Set a different printer as the default printer.

Unit 5

File protection and troubleshooting

Unit time: 50 minutes

Complete this unit, and you'll know how to:

A Back up and restore files and folders, and encrypt a drive by using BitLocker To Go.

B Troubleshoot problems, enable older programs to run in Compatibility mode, and record your steps to allow support staff to resolve a problem efficiently.

Topic A: File protection

Explanation

Windows 7 includes a versatile Backup and Restore utility that you can use to make backups of personal files or complete system settings. You can save your backups to a separate hard disk, a network folder, or a removable storage device. Windows 7 has built-in CD and DVD writing, so you can also back up your files to a writable disc.

Backup and Restore

With the Backup and Restore utility, you can:

- Back up the files for all users on your computer.
- Restore files that you previously backed up.
- Create a system image of your computer. This creates a copy of your system drive, which you can use if your computer stops working. Restoring a computer with a system image is an exact restoration—even your installed applications are restored.
- Create a system repair disc, which you can use to boot your computer.

Note: To use the Backup and Restore utility, you need to provide an administrator password.

Backing up your files

You can back up your files as needed, and set up a backup schedule that works best for you. After you set up Windows Backup, Windows tracks all new and modified files and adds them to the backup.

To configure automatic backups:

1 Open the Control Panel. Under System and Security, click “Back up your computer.” (You can also click Start and choose All Programs, Maintenance, Backup and Restore.)

2 If this is the first time you’ve opened Backup and Restore, you’ll see a “Set up backup” option. Click “Set up backup” and enter the administrator password. After a moment, Windows locates and lists all non-internal storage devices available.

   Note: If you want to save the backup files on a network drive, click “Save on a network,” browse to the network drive, and provide the necessary network credentials.

3 Select your computer’s writable CD or DVD drive or external storage device, and click Next. Windows prompts you to choose the default backup settings or your own custom settings.

4 Click “Let me choose” (if you want to select which items to back up), or click Next to accept the default backup settings.

5 Click Change schedule to set your own schedule for future backups. Configure the backup schedule and click OK.

6 Click “Save settings and start backup.”

7 Insert a blank, writable CD or DVD into your drive if one is not already inserted. If prompted to format the disc, click Format. The formatting process might take a few minutes.

8 Click Done.

If you want to disable the backup schedule, click "Turn off schedule" in the Backup and Restore window. To enable the schedule again, click "Turn on schedule," or click Change settings to update the schedule.

Once you have set up a backup, the Backup and Restore window displays a "Back up now" button. Click this button if you want to manually create a backup, independent of the backup schedule.

Do it!

A-1: Scheduling a backup

Each student should have formatted, writable CDs or a writable DVD with sufficient storage capacity. Otherwise, have students save backups to a location on your network, or perform an instructor demonstration of this feature.

If you prefer to have students save backups to a storage device on your network rather than individual CDs or DVDs, tell them to click "Add network location," and then help them find the network location.

Point out that this step sets a schedule for future automatic backups, not the current backup.

Here's how	Here's why
1 Open the Control Panel	
2 Under System and Security, click **Back up your computer**	If the Control Panel is not in Category view, you can access Windows Backup by clicking Backup and Restore.
Click **Set up backup**	Windows scans for locations where you can store the backup data, and then opens the Set up backup window.
Enter the Admin password	(The password is !pass.) After a moment, the Set up backup window appears.
3 Select your computer's writable CD or DVD drive	Or follow your instructor's lead to choose a network storage device.
Click **Next**	
4 Click **Let me choose**	You can choose which items to back up.
Click **Next**	To see the files that will be backed up by default. You can back up more or fewer items.
5 Click the arrow next to your User Libraries	To expand it and view the details. By default, everything in your libraries will be backed up.
Expand **Additional Locations**	To review the details of this backup option.
Click **Next**	To accept the current backup settings. A summary page appears, showing the backup location and the data that will be saved. By default, the backup is scheduled to run automatically every Sunday at 7:00 p.m.
6 Click **Change schedule**	To set your own schedule for future backups.
7 Configure the backup schedule as shown, and click **OK**	☑ Run backup on a schedule (recommended) How often: Weekly What day: Friday What time: 12:00 AM (midnight)
8 Click **Save settings and run backup**	After a moment, a message appears.

If the CD or DVD is already formatted and has been inserted into the appropriate drive, have students skip to step 9 when the backup process is completed.

The process could take a few minutes, depending on the speed of the computer and the storage media used.

If necessary, have students close the Windows Media Player setup screen.

Facilitate a brief discussion on backups by asking students how often they back up important files or how often they intend to do so from this point forward.

9	Click the message stating that File Backup needs your attention	
	Enter the Admin password	(If prompted.) Use !pass.
10	Insert a blank CD or DVD into your drive	
	Click **OK**	A writable CD or DVD must be formatted before you can use it to store backup files. Otherwise, you are prompted to format the disc before proceeding with the backup process.
	If prompted to format the disc, click **Format**	If the AutoPlay dialog box opens during the backup, close it.
	If prompted, insert another disc	When the backup is finished, a messages states that the backup has been completed successfully.
11	Click **Close**	
12	Observe the Backup and Restore window	It indicates when the last backup was completed and when the next backup is scheduled. You can perform subsequent backups by clicking "Run backup now," or wait for Windows Backup to run automatically on the specified schedule.
	Minimize the Backup and Restore window	Don't close it.

Restoring files and folders

Explanation

Restoring folders or individual files is as simple as backing them up:

1. In the Backup and Restore window, click "Restore my files." (This button will appear only if a backup has been made.)
2. In the Restore Files dialog box, click "Browse for files" if you want to restore individual files, or click "Browse for folders" if you want to restore entire folders.
3. Select the folder you want to restore, or browse the user folders to locate the individual file(s) you want to restore.
4. Click Add folder or Add files, depending on the prior selection.
5. Click Next. If you want to restore the data to its original location, click Restore. Otherwise, specify where you want to restore the data and then click Restore.
6. Click Finish.

Do it!

A-2: Restoring folders and files from a backup

If the previous activity could not be completed, perform a demonstration, or take some time to explain the restore options.

If the window is not open, tell students to open the Control Panel and click "Back up your computer" (under System and Security).

Point out the separate buttons to locate files and folders to restore.

Here's how	Here's why
1 In Windows Explorer, navigate to the current unit folder	In the My Documents folder.
2 Select the **My Projects** folder	
Hold SHIFT and press DELETE	To permanently delete the folder instead of sending it to the Recycle Bin.
3 Permanently delete the **Notes** file	(In the current unit folder.) Select the file, hold down Shift, and press Delete. You'll use the Restore feature to restore the folder and the file.
4 Activate the Backup and Restore window	
Click **Restore my files**	You're prompted to choose what to restore. There are separate buttons for finding files and folders. You can also click Search to quickly find a specific file or folder to restore.
5 Click **Search**	
Type **notes** and press ↵ ENTER	All files with the word "notes" in the file name will appear in the list.
6 Check the box next to **Notes**	You'll restore the Notes text file that you deleted.
Click **OK**	

Point out that this is an alternative to pressing Enter.

7	Click **Search**	You'll also restore the deleted folder.
	Type **project** and click **Search**	To locate the My Projects folder.
	Select the folder and click **OK**	Both items are displayed and ready to be restored.
8	Click **Next**	You're prompted to choose whether to restore the files to their original location or a new location.
9	Click **Restore**	
	Click **Finish**	
10	Switch to Windows Explorer	The My Projects folder and the Notes file that you deleted have been restored.
11	Close the Documents folder and Windows Backup	

BitLocker Drive Encryption

Explanation

Unfortunately, it is increasingly more common for removable storage devices and portable computers to be lost or stolen. Often, these devices hold valuable and sensitive data. By employing BitLocker Drive Encryption, you can be assured that your personal, corporate, or customer data is secure in case of a lost or stolen laptop or data device.

BitLocker Drive Encryption is a feature of Windows 7 Ultimate and Windows 7 Enterprise. If students are using Windows 7 Professional, consider using this text for discussion purposes.

BitLocker encrypts a drive to prevent unauthorized access and even protects data from any physical tampering. Your computer or removable storage device can be unlocked only with a specific password, smart card, or domain user credentials.

To enable BitLocker, open the Control Panel and click System and Security. Click BitLocker Drive Encryption and then click Turn On BitLocker. (You can also click Start, choose Computer, right-click a drive, and choose Turn On BitLocker.) You'll need to provide an administrator password if you're not logged on as an administrator. You might need help from your system administrator to successfully enable BitLocker.

BitLocker To Go

Windows 7 introduces BitLocker To Go, which provides encryption for removable storage devices, such as USB flash drives. So if you're taking important data out of the office, BitLocker To Go ensures that only authorized users can use the device.

When you encrypt a drive with BitLocker, you're prompted to save and print a recovery key. This is important—if you forget your BitLocker password or lose your smart card, you won't be able to access the drive. You need to save the recovery key in a location other than the drive you're encrypting. If you're encrypting a removable drive with BitLocker To Go, you can save the file on your computer.

You can decrypt a drive just as easily as you can encrypt it. In the Computer window, a drive already encrypted by BitLocker will display a Turn off BitLocker link. Click the link and follow the steps to decrypt the drive.

Note: It can take a long time to encrypt a large drive, especially one that contains a lot of data. Also, BitLocker is a feature of Windows 7 Enterprise and Ultimate editions only.

Do it!

A-3: Securing your data with BitLocker To Go

If possible, have students use 256 MB USB flash drives. Larger drives are likely to take more time than is practical for the classroom setting.

If students don't have access to a removable storage device, consider using this activity as an instructor demonstration.

Point out that in actual use, students should use a more secure password.

If students are asked whether they're sure they want to save the key here, have them click Yes.

Here's how	Here's why
1 Connect a removable storage device to your computer	The larger the drive (in terms of storage capacity), the longer it will take to encrypt it.
Close the AutoPlay dialog box	If necessary.
2 Click **Start** and choose **Computer**	To open the Computer window, which displays the internal storage devices and connected removable storage devices.
3 Right-click the icon for the removable storage device	
Choose **Turn on BitLocker...**	After a moment, the BitLocker Drive Encryption dialog box opens.
4 Select **Use a password to unlock the drive**	
In the first box, type **123bitlocker**	
In the next box, retype the password	
5 Click **Next**	
Read the dialog box	
6 Click **Save the recovery key to a file**	
Observe the File name box	The file will be saved as BitLocker Recovery Key, followed by a long alphanumeric key.
Click **Save**	To save the BitLocker key. You want to save this important key on a drive other than the one you are protecting with BitLocker. Because you are protecting a removable storage device, you can save the key on your computer. You should also print the key and keep it in a safe location.
Click **Next**	Windows asks if you're ready to encrypt the drive and reminds you that you'll need your password to unlock the drive.

Depending on the size of the device, this might take a while. If the progress appears too slow, have them pause the encryption, switch to the BitLocker Drive Encryption dialog box, turn it off for that drive, and then resume decrypting what had been encrypted.

Some drives might not show a lock icon.

7	Click **Start Encrypting**	After a while, a message box appears, stating that the encryption is complete.
	When the process is complete, click **Close**	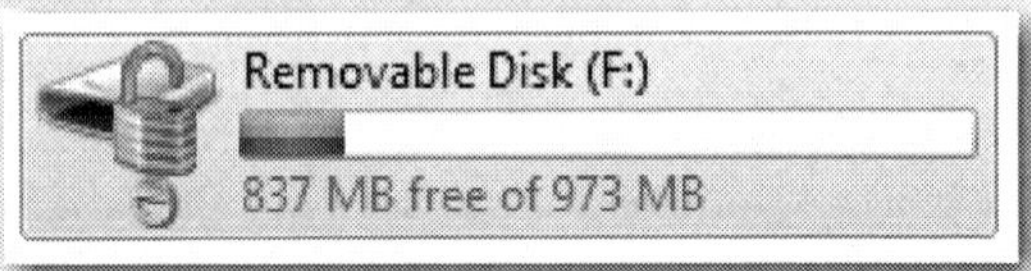 The drive icon now has a lock on it, indicating that any data on the drive now, and any data written to it in the future, is protected by BitLocker encryption. (Some drives might not display a lock icon.)
8	On the taskbar, click the "Show hidden icons" button, as shown	
	Click	The Safely Remove Hardware and Eject Media icon.
	Eject the removable storage device	
9	Physically remove the device from your computer	
10	Reconnect the device to your computer	The BitLocker Drive Encryption dialog box opens immediately, prompting you to enter the password.
	Type **123bitlocker**	
	Click **Unlock**	The AutoPlay dialog box opens, as it normally would when you connect the device.
	Close the AutoPlay dialog box	
11	Switch to the Computer window	
	Right-click the drive icon again	
	Choose **Manage BitLocker...**	To display options for this protected drive. You can change the password to unlock the drive, remove the password, add a smart card to unlock the drive, save or print the recovery key again, and unlock the drive automatically on the current computer only.
	Click **Close**	To close the Manage BitLocker dialog box without making any changes.

If students closed this window, tell them to click Start and choose Computer.

This step will take about as long as it took to encrypt the drive.

Consider facilitating a brief discussion on the importance of protecting personal and company data against theft or loss.

12 Click **Start** and choose **Control Panel**	You'll turn off BitLocker on the removable drive.
Click **System and Security**	
Click **BitLocker Drive Encryption**	Here, you can open the Manage BitLocker dialog box or turn off BitLocker encryption.
13 Click **Turn Off BitLocker**	 A message box states that this might take a while—as long as it took to encrypt the drive.
Click **Decrypt Drive**	Windows begins the decryption process, which can take a few minutes, depending on the capacity of the device.
When the process is complete, click **Close**	
14 Close all open windows	

Topic B: Troubleshooting

Explanation

Sometimes your applications might not work as expected. While significant problems are best left for your organization's IT staff, learning a few ways to resolve common problems can save you time and reduce requests for help from your organization's support staff.

The Windows Troubleshooting Platform

When a system device or application isn't performing as expected, you might seek help from your organization's IT staff. However, Windows 7 empowers you to solve issues before escalating them to support staff. The Windows Troubleshooting platform can automatically detect and fix many common problems with devices and application compatibility. Many problems are resolved transparently, requiring little, if any, user interaction.

To troubleshoot problems you encounter with programs, audio, devices, your network, or other areas, open the Control Panel. Under System and Security, click "Find and fix problems." (If the Control Panel is not in Category view, click Troubleshooting.) The Troubleshooting window opens, as shown in Exhibit 5-1.

Click a category heading for more options in that category, or click a specific option under a heading. Options that have a shield icon next to them are commands that require an administrator password.

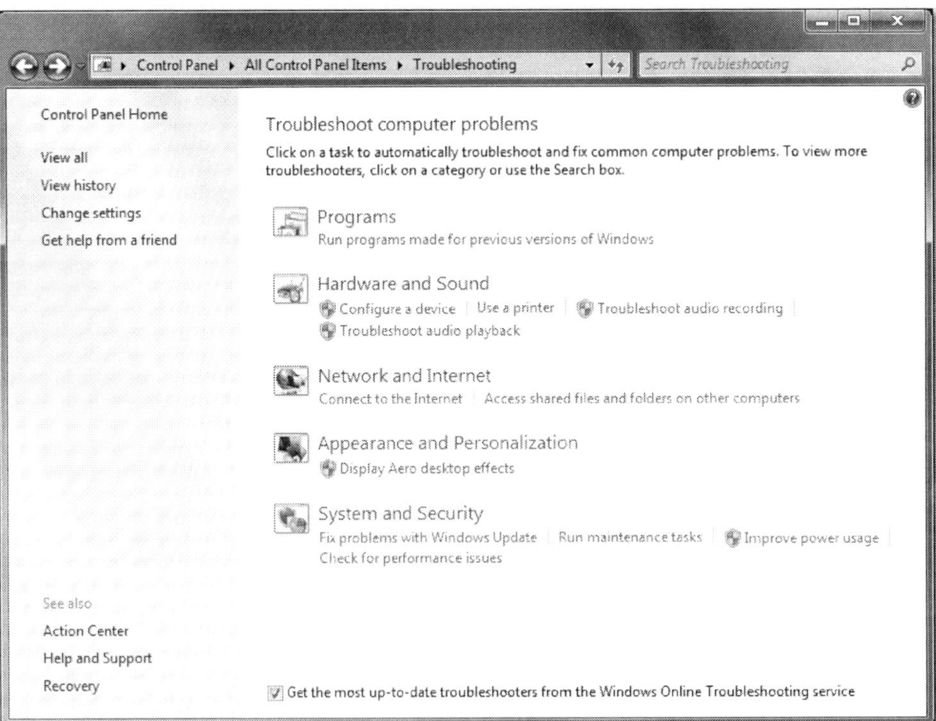

Exhibit 5-1: The Troubleshooting window

Do it!

B-1: Troubleshooting a problem

Here's how	Here's why
1 Open the Control Panel	
2 Under System and Security, click **Find and fix problems**	To open the Troubleshooting window, which lists several categories for problem solving.
3 Click **Programs**	
Observe the troubleshooting options	In the Programs category, you can troubleshoot your Internet connection, browser performance, program compatibility, printer, and media player.
4 Click the Back button	To go back to the Troubleshooting window.
5 Click **Hardware and Sound**	
Observe the troubleshooting options	In this category, you can quickly resolve audio problems, hardware and device problems, and network and printer problems that might arise.
6 Go back to the Troubleshooting window	Click the Back button, or click Troubleshooting in the Address bar.
7 Click **Appearance and Personalization**	
Click **Aero**	To troubleshoot the Aero display.
Enter the Admin password	
Click **Next**	Windows checks the video card support and other settings. If the Aero effect (the transparency of windows) is not active and your computer supports it, Windows automatically turns the feature on. If the feature is already on, Windows indicates that no problem is found. If your computer does not support the Aero feature, you are notified.
8 Close all open windows	

Point out that this is just an example of how Windows 7 automates most troubleshooting tasks.

Running programs made for older versions of Windows

Explanation

While most software originally created for Windows XP and Windows 2000 will run perfectly on Windows 7, there's a chance that some older software won't run optimally. The Program Compatibility Wizard can diagnose and fix many problems associated with older software so that it can run smoothly on Windows 7. This feature can prevent your having to purchase upgrades when an older program has all the features you need.

If an older program does not start or is not running smoothly:

1. Open the Control Panel and click Programs.
2. Click "Run programs made for previous versions of Windows" to start the Program Compatibility Wizard.
3. Click Next. Windows looks for programs that might have compatibility problems and then displays them in a list. (If no program is found, you're prompted to provide the exact location of the program file.)
4. Select the program you're having a problem with, and click Next.
5. Click "Try recommended settings." (Or click "Troubleshoot program" if you prefer to select a specific problem from a list of options.)
6. Windows applies changes and prompts you to run the program to verify that it works properly. After testing the program, close it and click Next.
7. If the new settings worked, click "Yes, save these settings for this program." Otherwise, click "No, try again using different settings" or "No, report the problem to Microsoft and check online for a solution."
8. Click Close.

Do it!

B-2: Making an older program compatible with Windows 7

Students will run Ad-Aware in Compatibility mode, as if the program were not performing optimally or at all.

Here's how	Here's why
1 Open the Control Panel	You'll configure Ad-Aware to run as a Windows XP program.
2 Click **Programs**	
Under Programs and Features, click **Run programs made for previous versions of Windows**	To start the Program Compatibility Wizard.
Click **Next**	
3 In the list, select **Ad-Aware**, and click **Next**	
4 Click **Try recommended settings**	Windows Compatibility mode applies the settings of Windows XP, Service Pack 2.
5 Click **Start the program...**	To test the new settings. Windows 7 is now making it appear to the Ad-Aware program that it's running on Windows XP.
Verify that the program started	(It should be displayed behind the Program Compatibility Wizard.) Although this version of Ad-Aware does work correctly in Windows 7, you can see the options you have for running an older program that isn't starting or working properly.
Click **Next**	
6 Click **Yes, save these settings for this program**	
7 Click **Close**	
8 Close Ad-Aware	

Remind students that this was a learning exercise. Ad-Aware already runs properly on Windows 7.

The Problem Steps Recorder

Explanation

Another way to solve problems and reduce calls for support is to use the *Problem Steps Recorder* (PSR). With this feature, you can record your interactions with a program or device and effortlessly create a detailed report with screen images and related information. This report provides support staff with the information they need to resolve problems quickly. You can also use these reports to build a database of common problems, which can further reduce calls to support staff. This is particularly useful for workers who are away from the office and don't have direct access to IT support.

The PSR allows IT staff to see precisely what steps are producing a problem or error, which makes the resolution process faster and more precise. The PSR automatically produces a zipped *.mht* file—a compiled Web page detailing every step taken, complete with highlighted screen images for precise reference. You can then e-mail the file to support personnel so they can resolve the problem efficiently.

To open the Problem Steps Recorder, shown in Exhibit 5-2, click Start, type *psr*, and press Enter. Click Start Record to begin recording, and then reproduce the steps or actions that are causing the problem. When you're finished, click Stop Record. The Save As dialog box opens. Enter a file name and click Save. Then all you need to do is e-mail the file to support staff, and they can contact you with the required support. You can also upload the report to your company's network so that other users can refer to it.

Exhibit 5-2: The Problem Steps Recorder (PSR)

Do it!

B-3: Recording and reporting a problem

Point out that the PSR can help students get help with any of the applications they use in the workplace.

Point out that because a problem does not currently exist, students will simulate the process by taking a few steps to produce an error message.

Here's how	Here's why
1 Click **Start**	
Type **psr** and press ENTER	(In the Search box.) The Problem Steps Recorder opens.
2 Click **Start Record**	To begin recording your steps.
3 Click **Start**	
Choose **Remote Desktop Connection**	To open the Remote Desktop Connection dialog box.
Click **Connect**	An error message appears because the Computer box was left blank. (This is just a simulation to demonstrate the PSR.)
Click **OK**	To close the error message.
4 Close the Remote Desktop Connection dialog box	
5 Click **Stop Record**	The Save As dialog box opens.
Type **MyPSRTest**	
Under Organize, click **Desktop**	(If necessary.) To save the file on your desktop.
Click **Save**	
6 On the desktop, double-click **MyPSRTest**	To open the zip file.
Observe the window	The compiled-Web-page file is given a default name, "Problem," followed by a series of numbers corresponding to the current date.
7 Double-click the file	To open it in Internet Explorer.
Scroll through the page and read the contents	The PSR automatically generated a complete report of the steps you took, with screenshots highlighting the areas of interaction.
Close Internet Explorer	
Close the zip file window	You would then e-mail this zip file to your support staff or post it on a network site.
8 Close the Problem Steps Recorder	
Close all open windows	

Unit summary: File protection and troubleshooting

Topic A

In this topic, you learned that you can use **Backup and Restore** to make backups of personal files. You learned how to schedule automatic backups, back up your data manually, and restore files and folders from a backup. Finally, you learned how to secure your personal, corporate, or customer data by using **BitLocker** and BitLocker To Go.

Topic B

In this topic, you learned how to troubleshoot problems. You learned about the **Windows Troubleshooting Platform**, which makes it easy to resolve many common problems that may arise, often precluding the need to seek help from support staff. You learned how to make an older program compatible with Windows 7, and you learned how to use the **Problem Steps Recorder** to generate detailed reports to help technical support staff resolve problems.

Review questions

1 With the Backup and Restore utility, you can: [Choose all that apply.]

A Back up the files for all users on your computer.

B Back up only your files and folders.

C Restore files that you previously backed up.

D Create a system image of your computer.

E Create a system repair disc.

F Reboot your computer into Safe mode for troubleshooting.

2 Windows Backup backs up which files and data on your system? [Choose all that apply.]

A Your photos, documents, and sound and video files

B System settings

C Installed programs

D Other users' files

3 When you're using BitLocker or BitLocker To Go, why is it important to save a recovery key and print it?

If you forget your BitLocker password or lose your smart card, you won't be able to access the drive unless you have a recovery key.

4 True or false? The Program Compatibility Wizard fixes unresponsive programs.

False. The Program Compatibility Wizard can diagnose and fix many problems associated with older software so that it can run smoothly on Windows 7.

5 How can the Problem Steps Recorder help you resolve problems efficiently?

By using the PSR, you can easily provide support staff with the precise information they need to resolve problems quickly. You can also use PSR reports to build a database of common problems, which can further reduce calls to support staff.

6 True or false? In Windows 7, many common problems can be resolved transparently, requiring little, if any, user interaction.

True

Independent practice activity

In this activity, you will configure Widows Backup and use the Problem Steps Recorder to generate a report detailing a problem you're experiencing.

1 Set the Backup schedule to back up your files every day at 6:00 p.m. (Don't perform an actual backup.)

2 Open the Problem Steps Recorder and record a few random tasks or commands. Then stop the recorder and save the file as **My Practice PSR**. Open the report in Internet Explorer and view the results.

3 Close all open windows and programs.

Unit 6

Internet Explorer 8

Unit time: 20 minutes

Complete this unit, and you'll know how to:

A Customize security and privacy settings in Internet Explorer 8, manage your browsing data, and use InPrivate Browsing and InPrivate Filtering.

Topic A: Internet Explorer security and privacy

Explanation

For many users, Internet Explorer's default security configuration is sufficient to ensure secure Web browsing. However, there are several new features and settings you can use to customize your browsing experience and make the browser's security more suited to your specific needs.

Secure browsing

Malware and identity theft are serious security threats. Identify theft can happen as a result of someone directly gaining access to the files on your computer, or it can happen remotely, as a result of a malicious Web site that you might inadvertently visit. It's important to use caution when browsing the Web, and ensure that your browser security settings are optimized for the kind of browsing you typically do.

The SmartScreen Filter

The SmartScreen Filter helps protect against evolving threats on the Web, such as phishing schemes. *Phishing* is the deceitful practice of sending e-mail messages to entice people to visit a Web site that is masquerading as a legitimate business or service. The ploy is designed to trick users into disclosing personal information, which often ends up in the hands of criminals. Phishing has become very common in recent years, and many unsuspecting users have fallen victim to scams and identity theft.

When you click a link to a site or enter a site address in the Address bar, the SmartScreen Filter checks a database to see if that address has been reported to contain malware, and it checks for scripting behavior typical of malicious sites. If a site you attempt to visit meets one or more alert criteria, Internet Explorer displays a page with a red background and a warning message about the site. It also provides a link to your home page so that you can easily browse away from the threat.

The SmartScreen Filter is enabled by default. If you turn it off, you can still use it for a particular site by clicking Safety and choosing SmartScreen Filter, Check This Website. If you encounter a suspicious Web site, you can click Safety and choose SmartScreen Filter, Report Unsafe Website to add the site to Microsoft's database of malicious sites. If it's confirmed by other reports to be malicious, the site will be blocked.

Domain highlighting

To help you verify that the site you're visiting is legitimate, Internet Explorer now highlights the domain in the Address bar. This feature is always on and cannot be disabled.

Do it!

A-1: Configuring the SmartScreen Filter

Here's how	Here's why
1 Start Internet Explorer	(On the taskbar, click the Internet Explorer icon.) By default, the home page is set to the Microsoft network, msn.com.
2 Click the **Sign In** link	
Observe the Address bar	The domain is highlighted within the full address so you can quickly verify that a site is legitimate, and not spoofed.
3 Click **Safety** and choose **SmartScreen Filter**, **Check This Website**	To check to see if this Web site is known to be or is suspected of being a phishing site.
Click **OK** and observe the results	This site does not contain any security threats. You can scan any Web site that you encounter, thereby helping to build a database of potentially threatening Web sites.
Click **OK**	To close the SmartScreen Filter dialog box.
4 Click **Safety** and choose **SmartScreen Filter**, **Turn Off SmartScreen Filter...**	To open the Microsoft SmartScreen Filter dialog box. You can turn off automatic site checking. With this setting, sites would not be checked automatically, but you could manually check sites that you visit.
Click **OK**	To turn off the automatic checking of Web sites.
5 Click **Tools** and choose **Internet Options**	To open the Internet Options dialog box. You'll use another method to turn automatic site checking back on.
Activate the Advanced tab	
6 Scroll to the bottom of the list	You can also enable or disable the SmartScreen Filter from this dialog box.
7 Select **Enable SmartScreen Filter**	
Click **OK**	To turn on automatic Web site checking.
Click **OK**	To close the Internet Options dialog box.
8 Keep Internet Explorer open	

Help students locate the Sign In link.

Point out that students can still check a site manually.

Point out that this is simply an alternate way to enable and disable the SmartScreen filter.

Security zones

Explanation

Security zones provide an easy way to establish a secure browsing environment. With security zones, you can implement your organization's Internet security policies by grouping sites together and assigning a security level to each group, or zone. By default, Internet Explorer groups all Web sites into a single zone called the Internet zone. This zone applies the Medium level of security, allowing users to browse Web sites securely, while alerting them before downloading potentially unsafe content.

You set security zones on the Security tab of the Internet Options dialog box, shown in Exhibit 6-1. To open the dialog box, click Tools and choose Internet Options.

Exhibit 6-1: Internet Explorer security zones

You can apply the following four security zones:

- **Internet zone** — Consists of all Web sites that are not included in the other security zones. This zone is set to the Medium-high security level by default.
- **Local intranet zone** — Includes Web sites on your organization's intranet. You set up the Local intranet zone in conjunction with your firewall. All sites in this zone should be inside the firewall. Obtain detailed information about your internal network from a network administrator. This zone consists of local domain names by default.
- **Trusted sites zone** — Includes Internet sites that you have designated as trusted. The Trusted zone is assigned the Medium security level by default. This zone is intended for highly trusted Web sites only, such as the sites of business partners or known, reliable public entities.
- **Restricted sites zone** — Used for sites that you do not trust. This zone is set to the High security level by default. When you assign a Web site to the Restricted sites zone, the browser can perform only minimal, safe actions. This security level might cause pages to be displayed incorrectly or to not work as designed.

The following table describes the security levels you can set for each security zone.

Level	Safeguards	Content	Appropriate zone
Low	Minimal safeguards and warning prompts	Most content is downloadable and runs normally.	Trusted sites
Medium-Low	Minimal safeguards and warning prompts	Most content is downloadable and runs normally.	Local intranet
Medium	Safer browsing, but still functional	Alerts you before downloading potentially unsafe content.	Local intranet
Medium-high	Safe browsing and still functional	Alerts you before downloading potentially unsafe content. Unsigned ActiveX controls will not be downloaded.	Internet
High	Safest, but least functional	Has maximum safeguards; less secure features are disabled.	Restricted sites

Configuring the SmartScreen Filter for the Trusted sites zone

While it's wise to keep the SmartScreen Filter on at all times, it does create a slight (and usually unnoticeable) delay as it checks URLs against the database of malicious sites. If you do most of your browsing with known and trusted sites, you might want to turn off the SmartScreen Filter for those sites only. (By default, the SmartScreen Filter is enabled for all but the Local intranet zone.)

If you compile a list of sites you trust and add them to the Trusted sites zone, you can then disable SmartScreen filtering for the Trusted sites zone, and add new trusted sites to that zone over time. This is more efficient than disabling the SmartScreen Filter for individual trusted sites.

To turn off automatic SmartScreen checking for sites in the Trusted sites zone:

1. In Internet Explorer, click Tools and choose Internet Options.
2. Activate the Security tab.
3. Select Trusted sites and click Custom level.
4. In the Security Settings - Trusted Sites Zone dialog box, scroll to locate the Use SmartScreen Filter option.
5. Click Disable and click OK.
6. Click Yes to confirm the change; then click OK to close the Internet Options dialog box.

Do it!

A-2: Configuring security zones

Internet Explorer is open.

Here's how	Here's why
1 Click **Tools** and choose **Internet Options**	To open the Internet Options dialog box.
Activate the Security tab	
2 Select **Local intranet**	Select a zone to view or change security settings. Internet / Local intranet / Trusted sites / Restricted sites
Drag the slider to **Low**	Security level for this zone Allowed levels for this zone: All Low - Minimal safeguards and warning prompts are provided - Most content is downloaded and run without prompts - All active content can run - Appropriate for sites that you absolutely trust This setting is appropriate only for sites that you trust completely. A local intranet is typically known and trusted well enough to allow all forms of content without prompts.
3 Select **Trusted sites**	By default, the security level is set to Medium.
Click **Sites**	To open the Trusted sites dialog box. The address of the active site is displayed. You'll add this and two other sites to the Trusted sites zone.
Clear **Require server verification (https:) for all sites in this zone**	You could leave this option selected, but there will likely be sites that you absolutely trust which do not use the "https:" prefix.
4 Click **Add**	To add the active site to the Trusted sites zone.
5 Type **www.microsoft.com** and press ENTER	To add the Microsoft site to the Trusted sites zone.
6 Type **www.bing.com** and press ENTER	To add the Bing search engine to the Trusted sites zone.
Click **Close**	
7 Select **Restricted sites**	By default, this option has the highest security level, to protect your PC from sites that could deliver malware or other unwanted content. You can click Sites to define a list of sites for which you want to apply extra security.
8 Click **OK**	To close the Internet Options dialog box and apply the changes.

	Step	Explanation
9	In the Address bar, type **bing.com**	To open the Bing search engine. Internet Explorer automatically appends "http://www" to the address.
	Observe the bottom of the application window	The green checkmark indicates a trusted site.
10	Click **Tools** and choose **Internet Options**	You'll turn off automatic SmartScreen site checking for all sites in the Trusted sites zone.
	Activate the Security tab	
11	Select **Trusted sites**	If necessary.
	Click **Custom level...**	Notice that the title of the Security Settings dialog box indicates that you're changing settings for only the Trusted sites zone.
12	Scroll down to the bottom of the Miscellaneous category	Near the bottom of the list of options.
	Under Use SmartScreen Filter, select **Disable**	
	Click **OK**	
13	Click **Yes**	To confirm the change.
	Click **OK**	To close the Internet Options dialog box and apply the new setting.

Point out that the options in the Security Settings dialog box can be focused to a specific zone.

Help students find this option.

Tell students to leave Internet Explorer open.

Clearing your browsing history

Explanation

For convenience, Internet Explorer collects information about the Web sites you visit and the information you provide to Web sites. For example, if you log on to a site, Internet Explorer can save your user name and password so that you don't have to re-submit the information every time you visit that site. However, if you don't want Internet Explorer to store such information, you can clear your personal information to protect your browsing data.

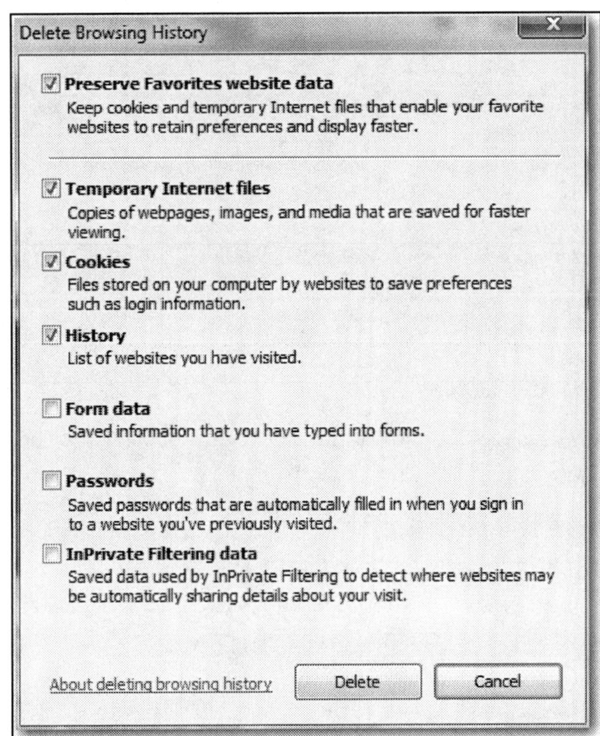

Exhibit 6-2: The Delete Browsing History dialog box

To clear personal information from Internet Explorer, click Safety and choose Delete Browsing History. This opens the Delete Browsing History dialog box, shown in Exhibit 6-2. You can use this dialog box to delete the information described in the following table. You can delete each type of data separately, or delete it all at once. If you delete cookies, you might be asked to enter personal information again the next time you visit a Web site that you log on to.

A convenient alternative is to select "Preserve Favorites website data." With this option selected, you can delete your general browsing history but retain all cookies and temporary Internet files for Web sites in your Favorites folder. This means you won't have to re-enter personal data for your frequently visited sites, and the temporary files allow those sites to load quickly.

To ensure that your user information for your favorite sites is retained, add those sites to your Favorites list. To do so, visit a favorite site and click Favorites. Then click Add to Favorites, and click Add.

Information	Description
Temporary Internet Files	These files contain images, scripts, and other Web site components. Storing this data allows Internet Explorer to load pages more quickly when you return to a site.
Cookies	Cookies are text files written by Web sites and stored on your computer. Cookies typically store user preferences and login information.
History	The History list shows the names of the Web sites you have visited.
Form data	By default, Internet Explorer stores some of the personal data you enter into forms. This data may include your name, address, phone number, and other information.
Passwords	For convenience, Internet Explorer can store the passwords you use to access secure Web sites.
InPrivate Filtering data	This data is stored so that you can track how Web sites use third-party content providers.

Temporary files and history

You can modify some aspects of temporary Internet file and history retention. Doing so allows you to conserve disk space, ensure that you're viewing the most recent version of a page, and control how long pages are retained in your History list.

Exhibit 6-3: You can configure settings for temporary Internet files and the History list

To configure your temporary Internet files and History list, click Tools and choose Internet Options. Under Browsing history, click Settings to open the Temporary Internet Files and History Settings dialog box, shown in Exhibit 6-3. In this dialog box, you can manage the settings described in the following table.

Cache is pronounced "cash."

Option	Description
Check for newer versions of stored pages	Internet Explorer saves (caches) copies of pages you visit to speed the display of those pages when you revisit them. You can specify when Internet Explorer should check for newer versions of those pages.
Disk space to use	You can control how much disk space Internet Explorer uses for its page cache. The recommended space is partially based on the available disk space on your computer.
Current location	You can change the location where Internet Explorer stores its cached files, and view the objects (cookies and downloaded program components) or files.
History	You can control how many days Web sites remain in your History list before being removed.

Do it!

A-3: Managing your browsing data

Internet Explorer is open.

Point out that these values are arbitrary and students' own settings will depend on personal preferences.

Here's how	Here's why
1 Click **Safety** and choose **Delete Browsing History...**	
Read the default selections	If you delete your browsing history, Internet Explorer will preserve the cookies and temporary files for sites in your Favorites folder. You can also choose to delete form data and passwords.
Click **Delete**	To delete the temporary Internet files, cookies, and browsing history for all sites except those that are in your Favorites folder.
2 Click **Tools** and choose **Internet Options**	
3 Under Browsing history, click **Settings**	To open the Temporary Internet Files and History Settings dialog box.
4 In the "Disk space to use" box, enter **100**	To increase the amount of disk space that can be used for storing temporary Internet files.
5 Change "Days to keep pages in history" to **10**	(At the bottom of the dialog box.)
Days to keep pages in history: 10	After 10 days, a visited address will not appear in the History list until it's revisited.
6 Click **OK**	To save your changes.
Click **OK**	To close the Internet Options dialog box.

InPrivate Browsing

Explanation

If you're checking e-mail or shopping for a gift on a shared computer, you might want to ensure that no traces of your browsing session are stored. With InPrivate Browsing, all the convenience features that save data about your browsing session are disabled.

There is no browsing history; no search data is saved; cookies are disabled; new temporary Internet files are deleted when the session is closed; and no form data is saved, such as user names, passwords, or other potentially sensitive data. Site addresses typed into the Address bar are not saved, either.

To launch an InPrivate Browsing session, click Safety and choose InPrivate Browsing. You can also open a new tab and then click Browse with InPrivate, or click "Open an InPrivate Browsing window." "InPrivate" is displayed in the Address bar, as shown in Exhibit 6-4. To end an InPrivate Browsing session, simply close the browser.

Exhibit 6-4: An InPrivate Browsing session is clearly indicated in the Address bar

InPrivate Filtering

While InPrivate Browsing prevents any traces of your browsing from being stored on *your* computer, InPrivate Filtering allows you to track and control how third-party Web sites record and share data about your browsing history. Some Web sites track your browsing habits and serve advertisements based on that data.

If you're browsing with InPrivate Filtering enabled, some content might not be displayed, and some pages might not work as designed. However, only third-party content that appears frequently on the sites you visit will be blocked. Content served by the site you are visiting will not be blocked.

InPrivate Filtering is off by default and must be re-enabled for each browsing session. To enable it for a browsing session, click Safety and choose InPrivate Filtering. To manage filtering options, click Safety and choose InPrivate Filtering Settings. The first time you do this, the InPrivate Filtering dialog box opens. To enable InPrivate Filtering, click "Block for me." The next time you choose this command, the InPrivate Filtering Settings dialog box will open. You can then customize the settings, see a list of blocked content, and turn off InPrivate Filtering.

Viewing privacy policies

You can easily view a Web site's privacy policy and the policies of all third-party sites active in your current browsing session. Visit the desired site, and then click Safety and choose Webpage Privacy Policy to open the Privacy Report dialog box. In it, you can see how many components make up the page you're viewing. To display the official privacy policy of each third-party site, double-click an item in the list, or select an item and click Summary.

Do it!

A-4: Exploring privacy options

Internet Explorer is open.

Here's how	Here's why
1 Click **Tools** and choose **Internet Options**	
2 Activate the Content tab	You'll limit the AutoComplete feature for added security.
Under AutoComplete, click **Settings**	To open the AutoComplete Settings dialog box.
Clear **User names and passwords on forms**	This is an extra security measure you should consider, especially if you share a computer.
Click **OK**	This setting will remain for all browser sessions until it's re-enabled.
3 Activate the Privacy tab	You can set privacy options for the Internet zone. By default, it's set to Medium.
Note the types of cookies that are blocked	
4 Move the slider up and down to see the other protection options	
Return the slider to the Medium setting, and click **OK**	
5 Click **Safety** and choose **InPrivate Browsing**	To open a new InPrivate Browsing session.
Read the default page	You can always verify that you're in InPrivate mode by checking for the "InPrivate" icon in the Address bar.
Close the InPrivate session	The original browser session is still open.
6 Click **Safety** and choose **InPrivate Filtering Settings**	
Read the dialog box	
Click **Block for me**	To enable InPrivate Filtering.
7 Click **Safety** and choose **InPrivate Filtering Settings**	The InPrivate Filtering Settings dialog box displays a list of blocked content (which is currently empty) and related options. You can turn off InPrivate Filtering, and choose content to block or allow.
Click **OK**	To close the dialog box.

Students will briefly explore a site's privacy policy.

If the msn.com site is open, have students scroll to the bottom of the list. The analytics.msn.com server provides a complete privacy policy.

8	Click **Safety** and choose **Webpage Privacy Policy...**	To open the Privacy Report dialog box. The list includes all the components that make up the page. For most large public sites that serve advertising, this list will contain several entries.
	Double-click an item in the list	To view the privacy policy for the company serving that component. (Not every item will have a privacy policy associated with it.)
	Click **OK**	To close the privacy policy and return to the list.
	Open other items until you find a privacy policy	
	Click **Close**	To close the Privacy Report dialog box.
9	Close Internet Explorer	

Unit summary: Internet Explorer 8

Topic A

In this topic, you learned how to use Internet Explorer's security and privacy features. You learned about the **SmartScreen Filter**, **domain highlighting**, and **security zones**. You learned how to establish security zones, configure the SmartScreen Filter for the Trusted sites zone, and clear your browsing history while retaining personal information for your favorite sites. Finally, you learned how to manage your **browsing data** and use **InPrivate Browsing** and **InPrivate Filtering**.

Review questions

1 What is phishing?

Phishing is the deceitful practice of sending e-mail messages to entice people to visit a fake Web site masquerading as a legitimate business. Phishing schemes typically attempt to trick users into disclosing personal information.

2 True or false? You need to turn on the SmartScreen Filter for each browsing session to protect against phishing schemes and malware served by malicious sites.

False. The SmartScreen Filter is enabled by default in all browsing sessions.

3 Which of the following statements are true? [Choose all that apply.]

A With InPrivate Browsing, all the convenience features that save data about your browsing session are disabled.

B To end an InPrivate Browsing session, you click Safety and choose InPrivate Browsing again.

C InPrivate Browsing prevents sites from recording data about your visit.

D To end an InPrivate Browsing session, you simply close the browser.

4 True or false? InPrivate Filtering prevents another user of your computer from observing your browsing history.

False. InPrivate Filtering allows you to track and control how third-party Web sites record and share data about your browsing history.

5 True or false? You need to manually turn on InPrivate Filtering for each browsing session in which you want to use it.

True. InPrivate Filtering is automatically turned off when you close Internet Explorer.

6 If you want to delete your browsing history, and you do not want to keep the temporary Internet files and cookies for Web your sites in your Favorites folder, what can you do?

Click Safety and choose Delete Browsing History. Clear "Preserve Favorites website data" and click Delete.

7 True or false? When you assign a site you don't trust to the Restricted sites zone, Internet Explorer blocks access to that site.

False. Internet Explorer prevents a site in the Restricted sites zone from using any active content and scripting, but does not actually block access to the site. Sites in the Restricted sites zone might not be displayed properly or work as designed due to this content restriction.

Independent practice activity

In this activity, you will add sites to the Trusted sites zone, and configure and clear your browsing history.

1 In Internet Explorer, add two sites that you trust and visit most frequently to the Trusted sites zone.

2 Set the number of days to keep pages in your browsing history to 5, clear your browsing history, and then close Internet Explorer.

Course summary

This summary contains information to help you bring the course to a successful conclusion. Using this information, you will be able to:

A Use the summary text to reinforce what students have learned in class.

B Direct students to the next courses in this series (if any), and to any other resources that might help students continue to learn about Windows 7.

Topic A: Course summary

At the end of the class, use the following summary text to reinforce what students have learned. It is intended not as a script, but rather as a starting point.

Unit summaries

Unit 1

In this unit, students identified the various **desktop components** in Windows 7 and explored the new look and features of the taskbar and Start menu. Students also learned how to use **thumbnails**, **Aero Peek**, **Flip**, and **Flip 3-D** to access specific windows when working with multiple programs and files. Students then learned how to use **Aero Snap** and **Aero Shake** to optimize the desktop for a particular task, and they learned several keyboard shortcuts for managing and arranging windows.

Unit 2

In this unit, students learned how to **customize** the taskbar, Start menu, and notification area, and they learned how to use **Jump Lists** to access frequently used items. Students also learned how to add, change settings for, and remove **gadgets**.

Unit 3

In this unit, students learned how to create and delete **libraries**, view a library's storage locations, add folders to a library, remove folders from a library, and change the default save location for a library. Students also learned how to customize **Windows Explorer** to arrange and display files and folders as needed, and display and edit file **metadata**. They also learned how to **search** for files and content, and save searches.

Unit 4

In this unit, students learned how to interact with and manage devices, and they learned about **Device Stage**. They also learned how to install a **local printer**.

Unit 5

In this unit, students learned how to **back up** important files, schedule automatic backups, and **restore** files and folders from a backup. Then students learned how to use **BitLocker To Go** to secure their data in case of a lost or stolen laptop or removable data storage device. They also learned how to **troubleshoot** problems, make an older program compatible with Windows 7, and use the **Problem Steps Recorder** to generate detailed reports to help technical support staff resolve problems.

Unit 6

In this unit, students learned how to use Internet Explorer's new security and privacy features. Students learned how to configure the **SmartScreen Filter** and **security zones**, and they learned how to clear their browsing history while retaining personal information for favorite sites. Finally, students learned how to use **InPrivate Browsing** and **InPrivate Filtering**.

Topic B: Continued learning after class

Point out to your students that it is impossible to learn to use any software effectively in a single day. To get the most out of this class, students should begin working with Windows 7 to perform real tasks as soon as possible. We also offer resources for continued learning.

Next courses in this series

This course is not part of a series. Our other Windows 7 courses are *Windows 7: Basic* and *Windows 7: Advanced.*

Other resources

For more information, visit www.axzopress.com.

Glossary

Administrator

A user account with advanced permissions. When logged in as an administrator, you can install programs, make system configuration changes, and create user accounts.

Aero Peek

A usability enhancement in Windows 7 that provides a way to see an open window's contents without activating the window. Pointing to a window thumbnail brings that window to the forefront and makes all other windows transparent, thereby giving you a peek at the window at full size.

Aero Shake

A usability enhancement in Windows 7 that provides a fast way to minimize all but one window. You "shake" the desired window by quickly dragging the title bar back and forth.

Aero Snap

A usability enhancement that helps you precisely arrange your windows on the desktop.

Cookies

Text files created by Web sites and saved on your computer to identify you or save login information for fast access when you revisit the site.

Default printer

The printer that programs print to by default. If only one printer is installed, it's automatically the default printer.

Device

Anything you connect to the computer, inside or out, for input, output, or storage.

Device Stage

A Windows 7 feature that streamlines device interaction and management via your computer.

Driver

A system program that enables communication between a device and the operating system.

Firewall

A system that prevents access to your machine by unauthorized Internet or network users. A firewall can be either software-based or hardware-based.

Gadgets

Small, specialized programs that sit on your desktop.

Jump Lists

Context menus that you can use to open recent and favorite files and folders. Right-click a program icon on the taskbar to open its Jump List.

Library

In Windows 7, a named collection of folders grouped for organizational purposes. Libraries aggregate files from various locations, including shared files on your network, and display them in a central location.

Malware

A general name for malicious software, including viruses, worms, spyware, and adware.

Metadata

Information that is about a file and stored in the file. It's "data about data."

Phishing

A technique by which people are tricked into divulging personal and financial information, typically through e-mail messages enticing people to visit fake Web sites that look like legitimate businesses.

Pinned icons

Icons that you attach to the taskbar or Start menu. They remain there until you unpin them.

Print device

In Windows, the physical printer that creates your hard-copy output.

Printer

In Windows, the software that manages the printing process.

User account

A collection of settings and preferences representing a user of the computer. In Windows, you access your user account by selecting your user name on the logon screen and entering your password.

User Account Control (UAC)

A feature that enables you to log in as a standard user and then provide administrator credentials when you attempt a restricted action, such as making a system configuration change.

Index

S

T

W